A Lifetime of Luck and Pluck

A Lifetime of Luck and Pluck

Bette Hammel

NODIN PRESS

Acknowledgments

Many thanks go to book designer, John Toren, who patiently accepted my verbal changes and made valuable corrections for his design. My editor, Caroll Pine, a busy author, deserves my lasting gratitude for her editing services over many months. I am also grateful to my daughter, Susan Hammel, for tracking down old family photos, and to photographers Karen Melvin, Joel Papa Sr., Jim Ingebretsen, Perkins-Will, and HGA. Finally, I would like to thank the generous donors who helped make this book possible: my Wayzata friend Renata Winsor and HGA Architects & Engineers.
Photo of Bell Museum: Correy Gaffer
Photo of Santiago Cathedral: CC BY-SA 3.0, https://commons.wikimedia.org/w/index.php?curid=54872
Photo of royal wedding: Unofficialroyalty.com

Computer consultant: Reed Wahlberg

ISBN: 978-1-947237-15-5
Library of Congress Control Number: 2018962192

Published by Nodin Press
5114 Cedar Lake Road
Minneapolis, MN 55416
www.nodinpress.com

Printed in USA

Contents

Introduction

Remember the popular children's song that repeats, "Oh, the wheels go round, go round, go round." It strikes me in my 93nd year, that is the way life goes too. My first chapter in this memoir describes how my many wheels carried me through life and then onto a career that evolved after graduation from the J (journalism) School at the University of Minnesota. It all began when I was a curious eighth grader and my dad, Whitey (Erwin) Jones, took me down to the *St. Paul Pioneer Press* where he worked as a mailer/printer. Over in the editorial offices I met a columnist, a few reporters, watched the linotype operators clacking away and all kinds of people bustling about. They all knew Whitey, with his mop of blonde hair and big grin. I loved the action I saw there.

My mother, Myrtle Healey Jones, a pretty Irish colleen with long dark hair, usually piled on top of her head, always took me to the Riverview Library once a week and I would emerge with an armload of books to take home and treasure. Reading was very important in our house, especially newspapers for Dad.

During those Depression years when I was born, my family was fortunate to live in the Cherokee Heights neighborhood overlooking the Mississippi River across from downtown Saint Paul via the High Bridge. There my little brother, Tom, and I could play freely and hike along the "Indian trails" on the bluffs.

Because Dad worked at the daily newspapers, we never had to worry about his having a job. His moderate income

The Jones family, 1939: Bette, Whitey, Tom and Myrtle.

meant that we lived in an attractive wood-frame house of two stories with a small back yard. Myrt, a fabulous cook, and Whitey were a happy couple who never had the advantage of a college education. But they stressed that I would.

After that trip to the Pioneer Press downtown, I told my parents emphatically that I would learn how to be a journalist when I went to college. It was an arresting moment for me and thus began my whole future career.

In browsing through my journal, you will learn about the original Betty Crocker kitchens, the value of train travel that transported daughters like me back home from other states, and how we ad agency women dressed fashionably though we were underpaid compared to men in the same jobs. The TV Cable series *Mad Men* was right in one respect: the 60s were the high days of martinis and glamorous office parties.

Sports changed too, especially my favorite, skiing, and even sailing, my husband's favored pastime. You will learn what Aspen, Colorado, was like in the early 50s, how European ski resorts were way ahead of ours, how ski equipment changed, and even how the scow-oriented Minnetonka Yacht Club accepted two fleets of keelboats.

It has always been a man's world in my lifetime. Even in architecture, it still is, although more and more women are graduating in design and engineering. In the ad agency business, women are often the leaders of their firms, though many now relegate high heels to evenings, and men love the popularity of the casual look.

With my grandchildren now in college and my daughter and her husband, Dan Broberg, making good headway in their respective businesses, I think more and more about the future and feel that it looks promising.

My professional career was richly varied with many rewarding moments, yet I hope you will glean the most meaningful parts of my life: namely, becoming a mother of Susan Hammel, stepmother of Anne Hammel, grandmother of Caleigh and Danny Hammel Joyce, and marrying the love of my life, Dick Hammel.

The wheels of life have taken me many places. See if you agree when you read the first story.

1
My Car is Gone

They didn't take the keys away. I did. (It was October, 2016). After the last eye doctor's remarks, I knew the time had come. I was doomed to live in a blurry world without my car.

Like most folks, I felt that owning a car was not a luxury. It was my other home. I kept my coupons in it, my extra coins, an old scarf (this is Minnesota after all), my water bottle, excess mints, at times my boots, the daily newspaper, a magazine (usually the *New Yorker*), extra bathing suit, even another lipstick just in case. I'll admit I was proud of my car. It was my alter ego and I drove it a lot.

After all, it was an Audi. A big beautiful bronze-colored station wagon. Yes, it was old. But like all old things, it grew even more beautiful in my eyes like the patina on a Summit Avenue staircase.

Sure there have been many different cars in my life. I still remember the first one, a broken-down Studebaker, but it was all mine, paid for with my own money. One morning something rattled and shook underneath the car. But I was determined to make it into downtown Minneapolis. The art directors at the ad agency where I worked guffawed at my story. No sympathy whatsoever.

"Bette, that's the crankshaft you're talking about," they said.

Another, "Get your skis off the top." Later, when I left that agency for another job, the head art director presented me with a gift—a framed original drawing of a tan Studebaker with a

crooked shaft underneath and a blonde pulling it with her ski poles over her shoulder. All the art directors signed the print.

The next agency job was a major promotion. Since I worked in the TV department on a household product, my boss decided I should go to the Hollywood studio where they would produce the commercial. Soon after I arrived, they handed me the keys to a gorgeous red convertible, the incredible Ford Thunderbird—the 1955 make that has gone down in auto history. Hot dog! I picked up a gal friend there and off we went, tooling down the California freeway just as though I knew the place. I've never been able to replicate the excitement of driving that rambunctious Ford.

I was also lucky with the next job. It was the late 50s when I landed a great P.R. assignment on the Minnesota Centennial staff and with it, a brand new Chevy. Shiny blue with Minnesota logo. I worked hard for two years, driving quite a few miles, but when the big events were all over, I had to give the car back. Not too bad considering this was one set of wheels I didn't have to pay for.

Next, during my first marriage, I acquired a little used VW Beetle. It was the cutest car ever, just room enough for my little three-year-old and me. My husband drove a beautiful red and white Oldsmobile convertible. No wonder that marriage didn't work out.

My reputation really went up in the world when I married again and my new architect husband was driving a Mercedes Benz. Well, it was a diesel after all. We drove around in style until I needed a car. I chose a Ford, just because I admired old man Ford who had changed the world with his Model T. This new Ford design was something different for the company, a Mercury-Capri, new on the market. It was made in the UK and did not have enough gumption so I traded it in for a different Mercury, just plain transportation.

After several years of a happy driving life, my architect husband and I planned a trip to Italy with our daughter, then 13, and that meant renting a car. We took turns at the wheel driving the Fiat. Fun to drive! As we approached Rome, I happened to be driving and my husband navigating. I thought the space ahead looked wide open and classical, but where were all the people? Suddenly, several Italian carabinieri came running up looking very upset. I stopped and rolled down the window just as my family realized we were not supposed to be driving there. "No one drives across the Piazza Navona!" shouted the policeman. "Ever!" My husband pointed to the hotel's name on our map and the exasperated policeman, waving arms frantically, motioned to the direction straight ahead. Okay. All was forgiven for stupid American tourists. I refused to drive the Fiat again in Rome.

We made one more trip to Europe before my husband died suddenly in 1986. My grief journey took a while but I knew getting back to work would help.

I traded in the now old Mercedes for a used Audi 1993

model. It turned out to be reliable for a long time but eventually it started leaking oil. That's when I acquired an Audi road car (2007) to begin the new century. This was the car that I really fell in love with. And it was all mine. I loved the way it flowed down the highway smoothly and effortlessly. I drove it all over the Twin Cities and as far as Madeline Island. I felt safe in it, thinking, *this is my "nest" away from home.*

But as my eyesight weakened, my eye doctors cautioned that I should not drive at night. That was okay for me. Ultimately however, the final day came. "You know, Bette," said the kindly doctor, "I will have to call the limit for you next year."

One week later I handed my daughter the keys.

No more freedom, I thought bleakly. No more sudden trips to happy hour. But soon friends, knowing of my blurred vision, came to my rescue. And better yet, my grandchildren and their young friends informed me, "You don't need a car anymore; you can just call Uber." When I looked dubious, my grandson, Danny, and Susan promptly marched me to a phone store where my daughter bought me an iPhone with an Uber app; then showed me how to use it. In a short time, I learned how I could go anywhere on this new app. Driving with Uber took me all around town.

I am no longer devastated.

I have fond memories of all the cars I once owned. And who else can claim driving down the Piazza Navona with Italian police scolding madly?

2
Must I Wear Glasses!

When I was an adolescent, about 13 or 14, I learned some agonizing news from my mother: "Bets," she said, "Mr. Larson says you need to have your eyes examined."

"Does that mean I'll have to wear glasses!" I cried.

No one worries more than a young teenager. Plus, Mr. Larson, my social studies teacher, was the one person in my whole school who liked my poetry. But I had to go to the dreaded appointment, and soon, before I could avoid it, I was wearing my first pair of eyeglasses.

"So ugly," I screamed. "They're way too big, they make my nose look bigger." (I had never liked my Jones nose.) Secretly, I thought, "Lou Guidison (the most popular boy in school) will never look at me now!"

At school the next day, I suffered through my classes enduring catty remarks of "Jonesy's got big eyes, why are you wearing those monsters," and finally, "four eyes." I was humiliated.

Soon, however, I had to admit that I could see the blackboards better, Mr. Larson wasn't quite as handsome as I thought, and best of all, I could read my favorite books better.

"You're just near-sighted," sighed my mother. Even my report card grades went up and I decided, well, maybe these little metal things weren't so bad after all.

When we moved to the countryside of West Saint Paul, I was faced with the horrible news that I would have to start high school in a brand new town, South St. Paul. (At that time West St. Paul didn't have a high school.) This was another blow. For a teenager like me, facing a whole new crowd of strangers my own age was a terrible fate. My mother, recognizing the situation, even offered to buy me new frames for my glasses.

My first friend, Harriet, wore glasses too (therefore we were considered smart girls) and it wasn't long before we were joined by others. Some of the smarter boys were even wearing them too. But not my idol, Stan, who would become valedictorian, and of course, he didn't pay any attention to little me.

My South St. Paul high school graduation photo, before glasses.

However, he had to suffer because the football players got the most attention from the prettiest girls. Privately, I swore that someday I would outshine them all, and wouldn't you know, it was the salutatorian, Ken, wearing the ugliest glasses ever, who trailed around school looking for me.

By the time I graduated in 1943, I was even proud to wear my glasses, and by then I sported tortoise shell frames— pretty fashionable according to the magazines. I still didn't get invited to the prom, though, nor did several of my "smart" girl friends. That was the final straw for me on high school. I was more determined than ever to become a noted writer, an author who that football team of heroes would read about some day!

Much later in my career path, I winced when I thought how vital my proper eyeglasses had been in every single job I had. New frames, usually quite the latest in design, became part of me, they stamped my appearance. I may have appeared as an intellectual to some, to others as an inquisitive journalist. Now I am very thankful for the eye doctors who helped me whenever the need arose. Opthamologists, we salute you! I am still reading and writing.

3
Gopher Days:
No Dates, No Men

Goodbye to Cow Town, South Saint Paul; hello to the Golden Gophers, University of Minnesota main campus, Minneapolis.

It was the fall of 1943 when Harriet and I nervously stood in line at Coffman Union for our freshmen welcome maps and class info. She would be a Spanish major and I was already prepared to major in journalism (with a minor in Spanish and politics).

The campus seemed huge to us, and we were awestruck even though only about 7,000 students were enrolled then. It's surprising how little we really knew about World War II, which had only recently ended, leaving thousands of young men our age either dead, wounded, or finally coming home. It was not until classes began and we looked around for guy friends that we realized, "Oh no, there are hardly any men here."

Happy graduation day at the University of Minnesota, 1947, with best friend, Harriet, on left, another friend on right.

At least we had some male instructors those first two years. My Spanish professor from South America was one, so handsome that I became his devoted student early on. The other was Dr. Mills, who taught political science, a course featuring the politics of India, which at that time was being governed by the British military. He was on the Brits' side. He was a small man with a slight English accent but he did seem to approve of Gandhi and the way he dealt with the poor.

Two years later, the whole campus changed when the men came back after the war (not all had seen actual fighting) and the University's enrollment shot way up to more than 20,000. We felt their influence right away in the Journalism School as many were experienced (also married) reporters writing for the Army's newspaper and other journals. Most of our journalism professors were males too, and they were special. My favorite (also my counselor) was a charming Scotsman type named Mitch Charnley. Learning that I worked at KUOM writing radio scripts for the Minnesota School of the Air (instead of the *Minnesota Daily* where many students worked) he encouraged me to major in radio journalism. Writing for broadcast, he reminded me, takes much shorter, snappier stories that help listeners visualize the action.

Creative writing was taught over in the grand old Folwell Hall, home of the English department. I can't quite remember the name of my English prof but I can still picture her. She was a tall lank woman with very long brownish hair wearing nondescript clothing. But oh how she could teach, fill us with alarm, and goad us into writing the best we could. I became so inspired by her that I wrote one of my best essays: "Life in a Pork Pack Department."

That story was based on my actual six working days in Armour's pork pack department in South Saint Paul. It was Christmas vacation and I was determined to earn enough money to buy a new winter coat, despite my dad's objections to my working at the plant. The place was cold, dark, and, most of all, smelly. My boss, Gertie, a tough kind of gal slightly older than me, was a little resentful of me at first, but as I showed that I could work hard too, she let down her guard. We packed those pork loins until our arms ached. At least mine did. Then when the bell went off (union rules) we trooped upstairs, sat on the floor and ate our bag lunches. It was the hardest work I had ever done, but I wound up admiring the people who worked there. How did they put up with this every day? I knew they needed these jobs. (I wasn't as tough as I thought, and wound up with a very sore throat; I had to quit on the sixth day.)

Though men were back on the University of Minnesota campus, our social lives didn't improve very much. We lived in a three-story rooming house in Dinkytown with a host of other girls where we all cooked and ate together to save money. None of us could afford to eat out. My roommate was another high school pal, Phyllis, (Harriet lived in Spanish house), and then Henie came. Every night I was busy typing my KUOM script based on stories I clipped from the *New York Times*. But my roommates seemed to suffer through that. Sometimes we would take a break and take the bus to a bar downtown where we could have a beer, although that didn't happen until we were of age in my senior year.

All in all, I enjoyed my four years at the U, especially working at KUOM where I was a little mad for one of the producers, an older man of charm and wit who actually liked my writing. Thanks to my job at the station, which broadcast classical music daily, I landed a chance to usher occasionally for the Minneapolis Symphony Orchestra at Northrop Auditorium. One of the most noted conductors of all time was conducting then, Dimitri Mitropoulos. I was thrilled to hear such beautiful music, and I have been a classical music fan and audience member ever since.

Before graduating, I was elected to the honorary society for women in journalism, Theta Sigma Phi. It was a big honor for me and proved that I had made at least a B plus (or 3.5 average). It was 1947 and women journalists did not seem to be wanted at the local newspapers. Only three females from the J school landed actual reporting jobs, while the rest of us wound up in various places where writing was needed. Luckily, thanks to my four years at KUOM radio, I landed a great job at General Mills in the Betty Crocker kitchens. That meant a good salary, a new place to live, and a desirable way to begin my radio career.

4
Stirring It Up
with Betty Crocker

University of Minnesota graduation, June, 1947. We screamed, we hollered, we hugged and cheered. It was a wild hot day in the Gopher stadium, with Judy Garland (somewhat sober) as our guest speaker. I was so excited that I already had a great job lined up at one of Minnesota's leading corporations, General Mills. Thanks to my writing radio scripts for KUOM, Dr. E. W. Ziebarth, distinguished professor and station director, had recommended me.

The Betty Crocker kitchens needed an experienced radio writer to help write scripts for NBC's *Your Betty Crocker* radio show. For my first day on the job I wore a proper suit and heels. I began learning the ropes from a senior writer, Mrs. Kenina (Ken) MacKenzie Kelly. She was an inimitable character, tiny and thin, with a beanie cap over her grey bangs and a watch dangling over her petite jacket. She confidentially informed me that she was not a home economist but that my job was to interview the working home ec's in the kitchens, find out what they were making that day, and turn that info into a five minute radio show. Ken taught me how to write dialogue as though the home economists were talking to Betty Crocker. I soon learned that Kenina had a rare gift for writing, along with a great sense of humor.

At that time, in the early 50s, the Betty Crocker kitchens were famous; here was the place where "Betty Crocker" created her popular recipes for loyal homemakers. Thousands of women came from all parts of the country to tour the kitchens, which were very expansive then. I had an enviable job watching these countless home economists at work, stirring, basting, mixing, and baking the most delicious cakes, cookies, breads, and pastries. Others were creating soups, main dishes with meats, chicken, fish, and vegetables galore. They were usually wearing crispy pressed white uniforms. While I watched, I would ask questions and gather tips for radio listeners about a particular recipe. Occasionally, I would get a chance to taste what they were making. The new cake mixes were just being introduced and I loved tasting the samples. The fragrance and aromas that filled the air made it very hard to remember that this was a job! Gradually, I learned which of these talented cooks could best describe her procedure. Then I would hastily retreat to my typewriter and quote what she had said. At the same time, I benefited personally, learning many ways to improve my own cooking.

Every so often, an imposing woman would enter the kitchens, led by a man from management, causing all the cooks to whisper, "Here she comes, our own Betty." I had written so much about her that I actually began to believe there was a real Betty Crocker but, of course, there wasn't. That was the ingenious name and image created by the leaders of the company. The first home economist who played the part to the hilt was Marjorie Childs Hustad of Minneapolis. My mother was disappointed, though, when I told her the truth.

The next year, my boss, Kenina Kelly, invited me to join her on a trip to Chicago to meet the NBC producer and cast of the show. Frankly, I was more excited to meet the actor who was then playing the part of "Jack Armstrong, the All American boy."

5
"Mrs." Jones on the Air

Your *Betty Crocker* went off the air about a year later, and Kenina and I were crushed. We were dimly aware that a thing called television was coming. Would it replace radio? Ken still had her post for ensuing years of work. And though I was offered a job to stay and write recipes for the cookbooks, I felt it was high time for me to move away from home and get more experience elsewhere. Fortunately, another friend in the company sent me a tip regarding a new radio station in Fort Wayne, Indiana, where they were just hiring staff. I wrote for an interview, hopped the train to Chicago and landed the job at $40 a week.

Back home again, I packed my things, said good-byes to my family, and bought a train ticket for Fort Wayne, a city I had never seen before. Radio station WKJG was owned by the city's morning newspaper, the *Fort Wayne Journal Gazette*. It had acquired a small staff, about four or five announcers and office help. They needed me to begin immediately as the station's continuity writer, a fairly simple job that I learned quickly, and I was just happy to be working in an actual radio station.

Several weeks later, the manager decided to try me out as a broadcaster. Knowing about my background at General Mills, he suggested that Charlie, a popular daytime announcer, and I should dream up a food program, talk about cooking, how to shop for good produce, and even give out recipes. Result? The *Mrs. Jones and Charlie Show*. Miss Jones became Mrs. Jones because I really thought that listening homemakers would not take advice from a single woman. Right away, Charlie and I made a good team. Once we asked listeners to send us their best recipes, the mail began coming in, growing by leaps and bounds. The station was very happy and found an appropriate sponsor. Wow, I thought, an early success! But I still yearned for New York. After all, every good journalism grad hoped to find a future in the Big Apple.

I spotted an ad in a broadcast magazine: wanted, a new woman's director at WENY, Elmira, New York. I couldn't help responding even though Ft. Wayne was a friendly, enjoyable place. A reply came quickly. They liked my voice on the transcript I had submitted and offered me the job. I figured Elmira was pretty close to New York City, so I accepted.

It turned out to be quite a switch from the Midwest to the East, because I soon realized Easterners were definitely not as friendly as Hoosiers or Minnesotans. WENY was an NBC radio station with a large listening audience. My job, as women's director was (I was then age 23) to conduct an afternoon interview show featuring various guests, local and out of town. I also created a morning show sponsored by a local grocer, giving out tips on how to buy good quality produce for home cooking.

One afternoon early in my tenure, I was bowled over when the program manager informed me that Bennett Cerf was coming that day. "What?" I replied. "You mean the president of Random House will actually be here?" Yes, he said. Minutes later, Mr. Cerf arrived. I was so in awe to meet this famous man that I could hardly speak. Cerf, sensing my stage fright, immediately put me at ease with his gracious manner. The interview came off well and I hated to see him leave despite my early trembling. After all, this was the man whose company published the books that I had been reading most of my life.

After a while in my new habitat, I began to learn about Upstate New York: that it was a beautiful state, Cornell University was nearby, the Chemung Valley just outside of Elmira was famous for gliders; Mark Twain lived and died here, also trains came and went regularly to the City. One weekend, I boarded the train and went to visit a college roommate whose home was in Manhattan. It turned out to be a whirlwind, a big birthday party, dancing and champagne, whisking around the city with a new date taking in the bright lights and the awesome skyscrapers.

I made another visit down to the City not for fun and games but to try to find a job. I had done my homework and called two of the largest ad agencies in Manhattan. Every creative director I visited was polite but automatically sent me quickly out the door. However, the last one, hearing my story of radio work, promptly informed me that television was new and exciting and that I should check with contacts at home, get some TV experience, then come see him again.

Shortly after that, I couldn't wait to leave the East Coast for good old Minnesota. And that helpful ad man was right, it didn't take long to find a junior copywriting job at BBD&O writing radio and TV commercials. It was certainly not journalism, but women were needed in the ad agency business and this was a good start with a decent salary. Whoopee! Now I could buy my own car.

6
Career Girl Takes on *Mad Men*

When television first entered the scene in the late 40s, I realized it was going to change the world. And it sure changed me, a radio pro of the 50s. I decided the ad agency business would be my best bet for my next job. Back in Minneapolis, in 1951, my first job was with a big national agency, BBD&O. Next was another company even bigger locally, Campbell Mithun. But at both those agencies, I was mostly writing and was not given a chance to produce the commercials I wrote because they were national accounts and my boss usually flew to Hollywood to produce them. (The one time I was sent by Campbell Mithun to Hollywood was for a Snowy Bleach ad, and the studio there actually lent me a Ford Thunderbird to use. Wow, that was a thrill and a half!)

My next job (we moved around a lot in this business) was at a smaller ad agency, Olmstead & Foley, where I was expected to produce commercials using the copy I wrote. There was no videotape then so commercials had to be filmed or staged live. I got carried away for my Holsum Bread commercials that required four actors to sing the jingle for exactly 60 seconds on camera. The actors sang okay but they kept going over the time limits, so we had to repeat. Finally they were "on air." Afterwards, the KSTP crew members were laughing their heads off at my silly lyrics.

The only other time I produced a live commercial was for Hilex Bleach. That one starred my local find, a good-looking model, Shirley Hutton. We managed to do well at WCCO's new studios downtown. Later, the station, recognizing her glamour and talent, gave Shirley her own show. Many commercials later, Shirley took up selling Mary Kay beauty products and eventually sold so many that she won a pink Cadillac, a new wardrobe, and was pronounced the nation's best-selling Queen of Mary Kay cosmetics.

The author in her 30s.

Luckily, a year or two later 3M came out with videotape. We quickly learned that it was a godsend for us in the TV world. Now we could rehearse the actors, and shortly afterwards, see the results—whether they were effective or not. We also had to line up experienced crews to shoot the commercials and rent studio time around the Twin Cities or in various TV studios.

Next, I accepted a very good offer from Colle & McVoy to be their new broadcast manager. Whee! I was now an executive, with an office and a secretary. My task was to jump-start the agency into the new media. My new boss was Tommy Thompson who sparked a creative storm that never quit—whether the client was hog feed, snowmobiles, industrial, machinery or bleach. He would often come sweeping into our little department with a request such as, "Say Bette, Can you get composer Herb Pilhofer to come up with a parody of that song, 'The Daring Young Man on the Flying Trapeze' for Polaris? Tell him we would hire the English actor who starred in that movie." I always loved calling Herb with an idea like that. Pilhofer was a jazz pianist from Germany whom I had often listened to downtown, and he was happy to get commercial business. He was a soft-spoken guy who became my friend over the years. He also composed the Guthrie Theater's basic musical theme which called the audience into the theater.

Another creative challenge I handed to Pilhofer was for Rath Feeds. How on earth could we convince farmers to buy this brand of pig feed? With help from a witty account exec and Herb, we came up with a dancing pig commercial. It was hilarious and didn't really make sense, but it sold lots of feed.

Thanks to the arrival of the Guthrie Theater in town, we learned that actors were looking for outside work. I was then looking for a man who sounded established and could project a polished voice on the air for TCF (Twin City Federal). When James Lawless walked in for his audition, I almost fainted hearing his beautiful deep voice. Tommy said, "Hey Bette, what a voice that Lawless has! Now I s'pose we all have to go to the Guthrie. You know I hate sitting that long." Or, on another occasion, "I like that ditty you found for Old Dutch, but why not use that sexy blonde friend of the client's on camera. She'd sure sell a lot of potato chips," Tommy exclaimed.

Susan leaping on the trampoline.

After 11 years at Colle & McVoy, I decided it was time to leave the rollicking, martini-filled world of the ad agency business. I had just married architect Dick Hammel the year before (1970) and wanted to work from home where I could take better care of my little daughter, Susan, age 6. Those were wonderful years in our woodsy redwood house when Susan and I began piano lessons together and played with our dog, Sukie, a Norwegian elk hound. Dick built a doghouse, and we invited the neighborhood girls over to jump on the trampoline.

7
The Ad Agency Strut

If there was anything in our outfits that we career girls were proud of, it was our shoes. They had to be high heels, of course, with polished pointed toes. We managed to strut along blocks of Nicollet Avenue while smiling, skirts swinging, and carrying purses that looked like men's briefcases—no matter that our feet were killing us and the panty-hose was slipping. We knew it was a man's world in the ad agency business, and we were determined to look sharp no matter what. In the 50s, hats and gloves completed the outfits. Fashionable hats were really expensive, though, and gradually they faded from the scene. But high heels stayed (causing many moans and groans later in life).

I remember one favorite pair. They were yellow with a back strap and not too badly pointed, nor high, but I loved them and they matched my summer dresses. We were careful though not to wear "sexy" looking tight sweaters or short skirts (jackets helped) in case one of the account executives tried to corner us.

There were times when male account execs found themselves in tricky situations with their clients. One time, a happily married account exec confided in me that he had a very sensitive situation with his client, and insisted that I travel with them to a Texas film studio, where the commercials I had written for this client were to be filmed. The problem was that the married client had invited a "girl friend" along. My job was to keep her out of sight when we arrived and figure out ways to keep her busy so the client would be too occupied with business to pay her much attention. Well, that worked during the day, but evenings at dinner, he consumed a lot of martinis and practically fell all over the blonde. According to what she had told me, she was working for the company for low pay, and agreed to come along to save her job. That was likely a typical situation for women in many other offices. Now, thanks to the #me-too generation, women at last are speaking out loudly and clearly when confronted with male sexual abuse. I never had such a problem in the various agencies I worked for. My male colleagues were always respectful and helpful.

Back in Minneapolis at a larger ad agency with lots of big clients I wound up in the broadcast department as a copywriter/producer. The new job required new clothes, of course. And Dayton's was within walking distance; consequently It was easy to buy a new suit dress (to avoid looking too masculine) and a two-piece dress with a gold top and gold and black skirt. I remember wearing that to a lot of TV production assignments where the camera crew always complimented me. (Later I realized it was probably a little too tight). My shoes were black shiny pumps with polished pointed toes (of course.)

Working for ad agencies meant earning a decent salary (for a single woman) and having travel opportunities. My first trip to New York came early in my career at BBD&O while I was writing radio commercials for Cream of Wheat. These were broadcast during a favorite national children's show, *Let's Pretend*, a program that I loved when I was growing up. The day came when my boss at BBD&O announced that they were sending me to New York to meet with the producers of *Let's Pretend*. On arrival, I was so excited about being in the Big Apple I could hardly speak. When the time came to meet the sparkling cast of that popular radio show, I was bowled over. To think that I, a lowly copywriter from Minneapolis, was being thanked for creating their theme song, "Cream of Wheat is so good to eat, Yes, we eat it every day" etc. etc. It was a magical moment in my ad agency life.

Another major trip came up after I landed a good job in the broadcast department of an even larger ad agency, Campbell Mithun. Several weeks into the job, my creative director called me to his desk and handed me an airplane ticket to—guess where—Hollywood! The assignment was that I was to produce the TV commercials for a major household product at the Hollywood studio where the famous Hamms Beer commercials had been filmed. Naturally I worried about what to wear, something inconsequential from my summer wardrobe, it didn't really matter. These big-time film directors were fun, friendly, and gave me the whole Hollywood treatment. And no hanky panky involved. It was during that weekend that they handed me the keys to a new Ford Thunderbird, the 1955 model that has gone down in history. Hot dog! It was shiny red with a convertible top, leather seats, the works. The TV production job that had brought me there was forgotten and replaced with the thrill of driving that incredible machine. I called a friend and off we flew over those Hollywood freeways just as though I always knew them.

It was a complete letdown when I got home and faced my used car, the same old wardrobe, and well worn high-heeled black pumps.

8
ON THE FARM

What's an ad woman supposed to do on the farm? And what to wear? That was the first thing I fretted about while packing for a trip to Fargo and the North Dakota wheat fields.

High heels? No. Pantsuit? No. Shirtwaist plaid dress? That will do, I thought, for the actual production, during which I would need to interview farmers bringing their grain to the co-op elevators. The client? The Farmers Union Grain Terminal association—"GTA, the co-op way," as we announced in our commercial.

What the account executive didn't tell me was about the fancy dinners and martinis we would be having at the hotel for two evenings after the shooting. It was the 60s, after all, and everyone knows those were the days of the martini luncheons. And how! By this time in my agency career I knew better, having seen how clients were treated over the top by thirsty ad men. And most of the time, they were men. Luckily, I had thrown in one dinner dress and usually stuck to wine. Hilary Clinton hadn't appeared on the horizon yet, so pantsuits were not really in fashion then. Inwardly I groaned about this trip; what did I know about co-ops?

The Fargo "film crew" met us at the airport ... namely a short little blonde guy with a shy grin and wrinkled pants who explained he was the art director for Snyder Films. So I expected a three-man crew. Wrong. We drove to their studio, a walkup in an old unnamed building.

There we met the film director himself, Bill Snyder, a big man with an equally big and slightly mischievous smile. He hadn't expected a female producer either. So we were both surprised and suddenly pleased.

The next day we headed right out of town to the first grain elevator on our list. It was quite a scene The grain rumbling down the tall tower, the wheat fields all around, the flat landscape under a brilliant blue sky—it seemed we could see way over the horizon. On meeting me, a blonde, sophisticated city woman with no suntan, the elevator manager gulped and said, "how'd ya do." I proceeded to ask dumb questions and soon he was completely educating me about the grain business and how important co-op grain elevators were for the farmers financially.

Learning so much, I felt like a real journalist instead of just an ad agency producer.

Also, I began to realize that Bill Snyder really enjoyed filming all this. He had an eagle eye for good shots and he loved to talk about the scenes he was getting. As the day went on, I learned about his early experiences shooting films for the Disney studio. Then after the war, he returned to Fargo and worked for WDAY-TV as head photographer and cameraman before finally setting up his own film studio. He loved North Dakota and its big open country, so flat it extended for miles, and especially when the wheat fields had turned golden and were filled with huge combine machines bringing in the grain.

On my second day out in the fields with Bill, he spotted a big red combine just sitting there. A little gleam came into those big brown eyes of his and he suddenly whirled around and said, "Jonesy, you've got to climb up there, take the farmers's seat and act like you're going to drive that monster." I stammered, "But Bill, I've got a dress on. How is that going to look, and what do you want this scene for?"

Bill insisted that then I would know how it feels to be in one of these massive machines. Okay, tight plaid shirtdress and all, I climbed up, way up, where I could see for miles ahead it seemed. We never really needed that shot, but it was sure fun for both Bill and me. We kidded about a movie titled "An Ad Agency city girl steals the combine jump seat for North Dakota Farmer Smith. Will there be a protest?"

For years, that red plaid cotton shirtwaist hung in my closet as a reminder of the good times we had with Snyder Films. Bill turned out to be the most talented film director on our list, winning many awards for some of our commercials and especially for his full-length feature about the state of North Dakota, produced by the state.

What I remember most about Big Bill was his lovable character, his ever-twinkling eyes, huge laugh, and always wearing a large movie camera over his shoulder. Martinis later? You betcha!

9
Schussing the Slopes

In the early 50s, joining the Twin Cities Ullr Ski Club was the beginning of my love affair with downhill skiing.

I had skied only once at Moon Valley ski area, near Shakopee, Minnesota, with two pals from BBD&O. "Oops," I cried, and suddenly realized that skiing meant falling a lot, then learning how to get up. I decided we badly needed lessons. Mary Lou announced that she had read about learn-to-ski weeks for only $100 at Sun Valley, Idaho. We could take a bus from Minneapolis, then catch a train in Sioux City, Iowa, to get there.

Within two weeks, we left town. It was a great adventure for us greenhorns, and after one week of lessons directed by an Austrian ski instructor we became intermediate skiers, even whizzing down the Olympic run. We had conquered Mt. Baldy! In those days, Sun Valley was already a glamorous place with people like the Hollywood ice skater Sonja Henie out practicing in front of the lodge every day.

Back home rejoining our Ullr friends, I went skiing almost every Saturday and sometimes all weekend. We shared driving with other members and headed for all the slopes: Afton Alps among them, or Trollhaugen, Telemark in Cable, Wisconsin, and other rope tow areas. There were few chair lifts yet in the Midwest. One weekend, some of the boys offered to drive North to Lutsen. Not one of us had enough money to stay overnight so we skied all day, drank beer, danced at the lodge, then drove all the way home. It was crazy, but then we were young and who gets tired at 23!

On one memorable weekend at the Telemark ski resort in Cable, Wisconsin, I accidently rode the lift with a woman named Ann Hall, and we were soon joined by a chap named Jack Dietrich. The three of us hit it off right away and we skied together all day. We also became town friends then, and fate conspired to help us remain friends for life. Jack absolutely would not join the Ullrs but he loved skiing so much that he proposed we invite two more friends and drive out to Aspen, Colorado.

Five of us piled into Jack's sedan, three women and two men. What with all our equipment, skis on top in the ski rack, boots and duffle bags in the trunk, lunches and coffee inside, we were tightly packed. Jack immediately called us "The Inti Quinti" and with his salesmanship spirit cheerfully announced we would be there in a few hours. (Mileage to Aspen was at least 850 miles.)

We were determined to drive non-stop to Aspen, although some sleeping interfered. Still we ploughed on. Driving the hazardous road to the pass woke everyone up, especially when Jack was at the wheel. Reaching the top elevation, 11,000 feet, was breathtaking, but now we had to drive down that dangerous highway. Finally we made it all the way to Glenwood Springs and at last to Aspen, then still a small village with only one chair lift. It was 1952 and Mrs. Willis's Motel had beds for girls in one room, boys in another.

We all signed up for lessons. Our ski instructor was a well known Austrian, Herbert Yokum, who taught us at Sun Valley where he kept shouting, "bend zee knees, bend zee knees." The chair lift had canvas covers because it was a long ride to the top where the intermediate areas began. It was 1952 and the ski style then was the stem turn, rotate, rotate, rotate, arms out. Everyone used long skiis, wore leather ski boots, and carried ski poles with wide baskets.

My ski buddies, Aspen: Jack Dietrich, Nan Holland, me, Ann Dietrich, Marsh Erickson.

The skiing was thrilling, our first time in the mountains. I was jittery when we began our first run but our instructor soon put us at ease, showing us how to slow down when necessary, and how to make wide sweeping turns as we glided down the blue run. "Yippee!" yelled Jack as he found his ski legs and reveled in the snow conditions. The next set of runs were somewhat harder but we made it. Now we faced the last part of the mountain—steep, rough narrow trails leading to the bottom. It had been a glorious week so we celebrated with beer at the Jerome Hotel, Aspen's famous landmark. It was New Year's Eve and I spent a crazy evening exploring the hotel with a L.A. film producer who I met accidentally.

Over all, we took in the whole Aspen scene: tall, handsome ski instructors, glamorous women wearing the latest Obermeyer ski fashions, suave Eastern college boys with or without their wealthy parents, and especially the town. In the early 50s Aspen looked like a village, with some shops, little bars and cafes, night spots where folk singers prevailed, and the popular Crystal Palace, featuring the inimitable Mead Metcalf at the piano. We fell in love with the town, with skiing, with the mountains; we were hooked for life in the ski world.

After watching a Warren Miller ski movie at a ski club meeting I became fixated on the idea of skiing in Europe. Warren was promoting a trip to Austria and I impulsively signed up, even though I couldn't convince any of my friends to join me. It was 1956 when we took off, headed for Badgestein, Austria. Nestled in the snowy Alps, it was the most charming little village I had ever seen. Everything was built of mellow wood, and flower baskets hung from every balcony. It was late when I climbed into bed and felt myself sinking into a feathery down comforter. The next morning we were called early to set off for the chair lifts with Warren and his bride and a guide. The Austrian smiling guide led most of us moderate skiers at an easy pace until we became improved and then followed him at a more advanced rate.

That evening as the group gathered near the fireplace, we finally became acquainted. Several skiers were friends from California, some from Boston and the East coast. Soon our Austrian hosts had us enjoying the traditional cheese fondue and an old dining tradition: whoever dropped their bread into the pot had to buy the next round of drinks. The Boston boys loved this hilarious activity, and dancing with us girls. Meanwhile, a more sedate fellow drew me aside asking, "do you like opera? We are close to Vienna and could take a quick train ride over and back. Want to go," he asked. I wholeheartedly agreed. The next morning early, we boarded a train to Vienna, and headed directly to the opera house for matinee tickets. I confess I don't remember which opera we saw, but it was wonderful and I loved the architecture of the famous Vienna Opera House.

That same day, we rejoined our ski tour just in time to leave for Saint Anton an Alberg, a much larger ski area. We had a very good instructor there, I managed to stay close behind him as we traversed, dipped, and swirled across the wide open slopes. We also skied Zurs and Lech, just over the next mountains. Good thing I had worked hard to improve my skiing because this was trickier going through powder snow. Whew! I felt I was now an advanced intermediate skier but it was then time to go home. During the trip I had acquired new friends, particularly Jane Dore from Boston.

Three years later, in 1959, I was between jobs and had saved enough money to take another European ski trip. The Alps were beckoning once again. I called Jane, she felt the same, and soon we had a trip planned. Another ski tour was leaving the Twin Cities for Austria that we joined. But first we planned to meet in New York at Kennedy Airport so we could fly together. I arrived in NYC on time, only to learn that Jane's plane was fogged-in. Result? After a long wait and a call from Jane, we decided to meet at our hotel in Paris. I boarded my Pan Am flight alone without knowing that this was one of their first flights using a jet aircraft. It was an almost vertical ascent that left me trembling. I calmed down only after the plane leveled off.

After my friend finally arrived, we traveled on with a stop in Berlin where I had arranged to meet a reporter friend from Denver now with Radio Free Europe. With his press credentials he could take us through the wall into East Berlin, which was then forbidden territory. It was an exciting opportunity. That evening, we met for the short drive to East Berlin, a place where very few tourists ever went. As we approached the forbidden gate, I was increasingly nervous. It was a dark night and the city looming ahead looked deserted, cold, and frightening. My reporter friend calmly stopped at a neighborhood bar, explaining that "this is where you can see what goes on here, but if someone asks you to dance, please say yes." We were seated for only a few minutes when a nice-looking German came over and asked me to dance. I jumped up and managed to follow his steps. With my blonde hair, maybe he thought I was German. Shortly after that, our escort announced we were leaving. We walked out immediately, drove through the gates leaving that darkened gloomy city. Later my friend asked, what did you think of it? My instant reply, "I never knew before what it was like to lose my freedom, but now I know."

After that harrowing experience, we were ready to go skiing and soon joined my Minnesota friends in St. Anton. There, Ann Richards (from Wayzata), Jane and I began taking our daily suppers at the train station café, where we met a one-legged Austrian. He asked to ski with us the next day which we did and marveled how well he could ski.

Davos, Switzerland, was next on my agenda. This was a huge area connected with other ski towns all over the mountains. I had to get adjusted to taking the gondolas and soon learned that while standing in line with my Head skiis, Europeans would trample right over them, while we Americans and Brits patiently waited in line to get on board. Then it was up, up, up to the thinner air where you could ski in many different directions. One day I opted to ski down the other side of the mountain, (easy and fun) and then hopped a train for St. Moritz. I still had time to ride the gondola to the top and ski down to Davos. Another time, I skied down the face all the way nonstop. It was one of the most wonderful ski runs I have ever had.

At night, the resort was teeming with skiers living it up. We happily joined in, dancing with so many different men we couldn't stop to count, but eventually ended with one each. My new friend Ann was with a Brit and I had partied with a Canadian, winding up in the hotel bar until at least three o'clock in the morning.

It had been glorious to ski in Europe in those days before the crowds. Ski equipment improved tremendously in the next decades. Plastic boots replaced leather, short skiis replaced long ones, even ski poles were different and, of course, our ski clothes changed too. No more baggy pants, stretch was in and jackets were streamlined.

And still I skied either at Lutsen, Minnesota, or in Colorado.

For at least a dozen years I was invited to the Oswald's ski chalet near Aspen/ Snow Mass, Colorado. There our generous hostess, Sally, invited about ten women every March for a week of skiing. Every day we drove to Snow Mass and absolutely loved the intermediate runs. Two gals from nearby Durango, Colorado, were advance skiers, and because they were ski patrol types, they made sure we got off the final run safely every day. Evenings, we collapsed: cooking, hot tubing, gabbing, and

Susan and I at 11,000 ft., Snow Mass, Colorado

sleeping hard. We continued enjoying the Owald hospitality until ultimately Sally fell ill and died during the late 70s.

A few years later, Susan and her best friend, Lindy, urged me to join them in a ski trip to Steamboat Springs, Colorado. Each Mom would bring along her daughter: Brook and Caleigh, so we would be three generations skiing together. I agreed to try it, even though my eyesight was beginning to be a problem. Caleigh was still quite inexperienced on skiis but after one day in ski class, she was raring to go. However, on reaching the top, I quickly realized that I was not able to ski that mountain. The sun and snow blurred my vision. The others, taken by surprise, then took turns steering me slowly down to the beginners trail in the trees. That was okay. I made it to the bottom and waited. And who should come whizzing past me but my own granddaughter, Caleigh, brand new skier at age 13. A proud moment for her Grams.

After that trip, however, I quietly hung up my skiis. It was time to quit. I think I was around 78 or so, but oh, how I loved every minute of my ski life.

10

The Spell of Spain

During one of my ski trips to Europe, I made arrangements to include a jaunt to Madrid where my University of Minnesota pal, Harriet, then lived and worked for the Spanish government. Accompanying me was my new friend, Jane, from Boston. It was the spring of 1956, a time when Spain was not yet as popular with American tourists as it is today.

I was not surprised that Harriet spoke Spanish fluently, owned her own little car, and took us around to see the sights. One major stop, of course, was the Prado Art Museum, with its impressive collection of works by Valázquez, Goya, and El Greco. The other even bigger attraction was a bullfight featuring the leading matadors of Spain, who fought in the city's huge semi-circular arena.

Taking our seats, I gasped at the spectacle, such color around the ring, the excited fashionably-dressed crowd, followed by the parade of the matadors, picadores, and banderillas, all brightly attired. We knew that a bull would be killed, but I had to admit the preliminaries were thrilling to watch. The matador was handsome, sleekly athletic, wearing a tight, elaborate, gold-encrusted suit and carrying a gold and magenta cape, later exchanged for a smaller red cape. We knew he must have the skill to carry out his mission.

We did not wait for the killing scene, however.

Next, Harriet announced we were going to drive to a city further north, Santiago de Compostela, home of a landmark cathedral, and the autonomous community known as Galicia, the verdant part of Spain near the Atlantic. This was the 1950s when very few Spanish women were ever seen driving cars, let alone American women. Along the route, we stopped at a hotel overnight. After checking in, we returned to the lobby and relaxed. About then, a group of Spanish men walked in and also registered. They took seats and immediately began looking us over. Noting that our dark-haired friend, Harriet, spoke the language, the group leader approached her, relating politely that his group was going to a private arena where their young matador, Fermin Murillo, would practice with the new young bulls. "Would you American ladies like to join us for this event?" asked the older man. All three of us thought this would be wonderful and accepted.

The next morning, we followed their cars, and relatively soon, arrived at the gates of what seemed to be an expansive ancestral home, including a bull ring and two bleachers. Actually, as we learned later, this was a large ranch where bulls were bred for the ring. We were immediately led to the "mansion" where we were greeted in Spanish by a smiling older gentleman (the Don or owner), and his wife. They were exceedingly gracious. We were seated with the matador, his crew and the family for a delicious dinner. Meanwhile, Murillo kept smiling at Jane, a very pretty well-bred East Coaster, who smiled at everyone, not just at him. Harriet kept the conversation going for us and I tried out my old college Spanish.

Following the meal, the Senora indicated that we should follow her to the ring, where the women sit on one side, the men on the other. Soon the action began. I could tell that Murillo was like any youthful up-and-coming star in training, and from what we could see he did pretty well with his cape maneuvers thrusting at the young bulls. We felt so privileged just to witness this and thanked our hosts over and over as best we could.

For the last few days of exploring Spain, Harriet continued our drive to the northwestern coast, to Santiago de Compostela, and its famous cathedral. It was constructed by an architect/master builder who designed its unique three Baroque spires in the form of the Latin cross. The style was originally Romanesque but over the years Gothic, Baroque and neo-classical features were added. The cathedral is famously reputed to be the burial place of Saint James, one of Christ's 12 apostles: therefore, it has become a renown pilgrimage

The Cathedral of Santiago de Compostela

destination for people who walk the 500-mile Camino route through northern Spain. We were fortunate to have seen this notable place and one of Europe's most famous cathedrals.

Then it was time for Jane and me to head for the Madrid airport and home. My old friend Harriet ended her time in Spain in a romance with a high-ranking officer of the Spanish Army. He proposed, but she said she wasn't ready for marriage, and when her term of employment was completed she soon flew back to Minnesota. The suitor did not give up. A few months later, the Colonel flew to South Saint Paul, Minnesota, to meet her family. Still, she remained unconvinced, knowing that as much as she had enjoyed living in Spain, she wanted to spend the rest of her life in the U.S. The disappointed officer politely thanked her family (who had originally come from Yugoslavia) for their hospitality and returned to his regiment. Jane flew home to Boston where she soon wed her current beau, and yours truly—this career girl—went back to work.

11
Grace Kelly and Me

It was big news in 1956 that Hollywood star and socialite Grace Kelly was going to marry the Prince of Monaco at Easter time. I perked up right away because I was going on a ski trip to Europe about the same time and thought I could figure out a way to see the wedding festivities. It would just mean squeezing in a side trip to Monaco. The plan was to meet my Boston friend, Jane Powers, in Paris, then fly to Austria to join other friends skiing in the Alps. After the skiing in Switzerland, I would leave my friends and board another flight to meet an Elmira friend, Ester, In Rome. Because I was planning the itinerary, I decided we should go to Monte Carlo from there and join the celebration.

All those years in the Journalism School had taught me how to act like a journalist—be nosy, be aggressive. Besides, I knew how to use my uncle's 16mm movie camera for ski movies. Maybe I could pretend to be a TV photo specialist. That settled, before leaving I went to WCCO-TV where I knew Dave Moore's assistant and asked for a press card. He knew I was a J School graduate, but what he didn't know was that I had never worked as a journalist, only as an advertising copywriter. He immediately gave me the card, impressed that I was going to be in Monte Carlo for that big date.

Shortly after we arrived, we approached the press tent on the hillside of the palace. I introduced Ester as my "photographer." (She was a rather shy, quiet woman, not at all like me but willing to play along.) We were given press registration right away and then a nice B&B for lodging. Wow, were we ever lucky with that, as the whole city was jammed.

At the press tent, I was approached by an excited Italian camera crew of three. The leader, speaking in broken English, asked if I could help them interpret a letter they wanted to send to Grace Kelly's mother before the wedding. I replied in my best college Spanish/Italian/English, stammering that I could try. "Bravo," they replied and handed me their letter. I asked for a typewriter and valiantly tried to create such a letter. After at least an hour, I showed them the result. They seemed pleased and turned it over to the authorities in the press tent. I never knew whether it got through.

The marriage was scheduled the next day in the little French church on top of the hill. We scooted over there asap, elbowed our way through the media crowd and got in line outside the church entrance. I lined up my uncle's movie camera and waited for the supreme moment. Suddenly, the smiling bride and groom appeared, thrilling us onlookers with their happiness: Princess Grace, the American bride beautiful in a breathtaking pristine white jeweled wedding gown, followed by Prince Rainier, tall, dark, and distinguished in his monarchial uniform. Flash! A thousand camera bulbs went off while I quickly aimed for my shots. I got one of the couple seated in their open limo, and another as the procession turned to drive down the winding hill.

Sadly, it was all over too soon, but I knew I had a job to do. I had to figure out how to package my film and send it back stamped priority to WCCO-TV in Minneapolis. Unfortunately, there was no one left in the press tent to help me and, as a neophyte journalist, I didn't really know the correct way to do this. I should have asked the cameraman at the station before I left. Much later, I learned that it had reached the station, but was too late. It was no longer news worthy. (Sob)

Meanwhile, we bumped into our Italian friends who promptly invited us to join them at the Casino that evening.

I got excited all over again. This was the most famous gambling casino in all of Europe. So we rushed home, rested and tried to dress for the glamorous occasion. (All I had was an apricot-colored matching blouse, skirt and sash which had served me well before.) Ester had brought a dress along.

So off we went. Found the Italians and had a fantastic evening downing champagne and laughing at their jokes while taking in the colorful crowd—women in gorgeous gowns, men in tuxes, journalists in their usual garb and endless Europeans and Americans busily gambling away.

I felt like I had crashed a terrific party, playing my part as a pseudo-journalist, and having the time of my life.

12
Minnesota's Centennial Blast: You Betcha!

It was quite a letdown getting home from Europe and all the great adventures I had, but we career girls knew the best thing to do when facing adversity was to find a new job. I started looking for something that used the public relations skills I had acquired quite naturally while hanging out with ad agency types.

I soon learned that the State of Minnesota was planning to celebrate its 100th anniversary in a big way in 1958. Wow! I thought, that sounds like an opportunity for yours truly.

I checked around, learned that a Centennial Commission had been formed and jobs were being filled. Obviously I needed a good contact and I had one. None other than the former U.S. Ambassador to Denmark, Eugenie Anderson. I had worked for her during her ill-fated campaign for the U.S. Senate against Eugene McCarthy. I had gained a lot of savvy, political and otherwise, during my two-week stint in Red Wing living at the Anderson home and working with the editor of the Red Wing newspaper where we produced a special edition about Eugenie and her background. I admired her in every way—for her warmth, her poise, speaking ability, intelligence and charm. To my mind, that meant she had a good chance of winning. But it was not the right time in history and McCarthy proved to be a witty and effective senator with a crowd of loyal fans. I met with Eugenie and she promptly recommended me to the public affairs director of the Centennial, Don Padilla, who became my public relations mentor in later years. He hired me right off, even though I called him "the slave-driver."

A sporty guy, Bob Reed, and I were "It" in the Centennial public relations department. We worked day and night; it was challenging fast-changing work and I loved it. Besides,

we were each given a brand new Chevy to drive and I had never felt so fortunate, even though almost all our mileage was piled up with business assignments. Tom Swain, executive director of the Centennial, worked equally hard that year along with Padilla and his partner, Dave Speer.

Padilla taught me how to think big when planning special events. He and Dave dreamed up arranging for a Centennial train that traveled from St. Paul to Duluth with various cars filled with the wondrous works of all Minnesotans, ranging from agricultural products to Native American handicrafts, the arts and culture of the Twin Cities, sports and athletics, the University of Minnesota, leading corporations and industry. Special celebrities were invited along. We also produced a Centennial cookbook, using my mother's teakettle on the cover and hiring my journalism school friend Ginny Huck to collect all the recipes and write the book.

The biggest assignment for me that summer was to work with the NBC *Today Show* writers. It was fun meeting them, but I quickly realized they were just a bunch of bored New

Yorkers who thought they had just hit cow country. They began to brighten up as I drove them around some of the Twin Cities lakes, and especially when I pulled over along Lake of the Isles and said, "Here is your spot for the broadcast." I had chosen a wide open public space nicely landscaped with trees and flowers, and they became gleeful. All three jumped out and began planning just where the cameras should be, where the program host Dave Garroway should sit, and how the lighting would work. Meeting Dave Garroway was a highlight for me after watching his show for several years. He was quite a jovial and friendly guy. I also did a lot of research for the writers to use in describing Minnesota, land of 10,000 lakes, and the history of the local lake where the broadcast would be originating.

It had to be a live broadcast, of course, in those days before video tape, so we were all a little nervous when they went on the air. Once Garroway got started in his genial way, he welcomed viewers all over America, informing them that "this is Minnesota, land of the fabulous 10,000 lakes and it is beautiful here." I was ready to celebrate after that.

Before the NBC crew left, there was a big farewell dinner where they publicly thanked me for all my work, giving me a big round of applause. That was a wonderful and unexpected surprise.

13
Enter the Kennedy Era

It must have been those midnight talks with my dad that convinced me to become a Democrat. Once he became a member of the union, the ITU (International Typographical Union) his pay was substantially increased. That is why I have always been in favor of labor unions.

I was in my 30s and living in Kenwood when I joined the Young Democrats. (There was a young Republican group too, a good thing for both parties.) With several friends, I became more and more involved in campaigns. One year, we worked very hard to help Orville Freeman win his election as Minnesota's governor. Thanks to my advertising background, I was asked to counsel Jane Freeman, his wife, for her TV appearances. Through my various involvements, I was officially elected as Minnesota's YDFL National Committeewoman to the national convention of Young Democrats in Oklahoma in 1961.

All over Minneapolis, politics was in the air with the Democratic National Convention soon to be held in California. I was itching to go so I asked a media friend for a press pass. My neighborhood, Kenwood, seemed to be rife with parties at that time, especially in the 7th ward. Joan Mondale was our precinct chair and Walter Mondale our state attorney general, and later U.S. vice president. I learned that there was still room for me to join the DFL delegation on the plane headed for California. With that pass, I was entitled to walk around the convention floor rubbing elbows with famous journalists and politicians from all over the world. It was so exciting!

Our Minnesota delegation was split, half for Adlai Stevenson, half for John F. Kennedy. We had heard Adlai speak and admired him as an intellectual while we didn't know much about JFK.

Our well-known Minnesota senator, Eugene McCarthy, gave a moving speech nominating Stevenson, while our popular governor, Orville Freeman, delivered a rip-roaring nomination for Kennedy. The crowd burst into cheers with every delegation shouting "We want Kennedy." Lyndon Johnson was then moved and voted as JKF's vice presidential candidate. You know the rest.

During those turbulent times, I had met, dated, and married a dashing young DFLer, John Munro, who was a busy Xerox salesman Our marriage succeeded for a few years but problems emerged and we eventually divorced.

Fortunately, however, I had become pregnant. On August 2, 1964, after an early morning race to the hospital, my beautiful blonde baby girl, Susan, was born prematurely and perfectly. It was the most thrilling moment of my life. I was a 39-year-old mom, unusual for those times—not so now. I arranged for a year's leave of absence from my job so I could take care of my own baby and learn more about child care.

By then we had moved into a small house in the woods of Minnetonka, west of Minneapolis. We loved its modernist design and the way it sat so comfortably on its woodsy site. Despite my best efforts, my marriage came to an end. I hired a very good babysitter who came to the house for my little daughter and then I went back to work. In my spare time, I continued to be active in Democratic politics.

In 1963, our handsome young president, John F. Kennedy, was shot and killed in Dallas, a terrible incident that sent the whole nation into grieving. However, in 1977, Jimmy Carter was elected president and our friend Walter Mondale became vice president. They carried on substantially well for four years. Then Reagan ran and was easily elected. Four years later, Mondale decided to run for president himself, thinking that the Democrats might make a comeback.

While he and Joan were campaigning, Minnesota Democrats were asked to help. A bright PR woman in town jumped in to head the publicity staff and asked me to volunteer assistance. That meant being trained as an advance person for the campaign. In 1971, I did my first tour leading Joan Mondale at a rally in a Minnesota town. Then came the big time. I was sent to Collegeville, Texas, where I met with the local Democratic leaders, then toured the site where Mrs. Mondale was scheduled to speak, then went to the airport to escort Joan into the auditorium. My adrenaline went way up. I had to greet the press, herd them into a certain space, make sure they knew where the telephones were and then introduce Joan to the local leaders. She spoke very well, then she was rushed off to her plane. Whew! Advancing candidates was not a job for me, I decided. Later, when Mondale was appointed U.S. ambassador to Japan, Joan became famous there for her work as a potter and her deep knowledge of the arts world.

Although I have carried on my interest in Democratic politics, I have had no real involvement since those early years except for a few scattered fundraisers. In recent years, however, I've been happy to see more and more women running for office. Many are also busy career women balancing homes and families. One example is Minneapolitan Margaret Anderson Kelliher, an unsuccessful DFL candidate for Congress in her district in 2018. As former Speaker of the House in the Minnesota legislature, she is well qualified and many of us "senior" democrats believe her time will come again. There is no age limit in retaining a major interest in politics, an important function of our democracy.

14
A Cozy House in the Woods

Amidst a grove of big old elms and oaks, the little cedar-clad contemporary house sat comfortably tucked into a hillside overlooking a wild marsh. Originally designed by Minneapolis architect Elizabeth Close, the simple split-level structure, with its weathered grey façade and projecting shed roof, fit into its woodsy environment as though it belonged. Modernist architects, though criticized for their glass boxes, really knew how to design homes that fit their sites. Our house in Minnetonka, Minnesota, was one.

When we first stepped into the house one soft autumn day in 1963, I was immediately taken by the sight of a cushioned window-seat placed alongside a rustic brick fireplace, which offered a splendid view of slender aspen trees just turning golden yellow.

The Wood Lane house

The living room, about 10 x 18 and entirely paneled in cedar, was not just a living room but what architects call a "great room" with space for conversing, reading, dining, and entertaining all in one. To the west, sliding glass doors provided a view of the woods and marsh beyond a narrow strip of lawn.

The kitchen was open too, placed at right angles to the great room but with a partial wall hiding the refrigerator, stove, and a sink area looking down towards the swamp. A small dining table looked into the living room. To add a more spacious effect, the architect had wisely provided a higher ceiling on that end of the room by transforming a flat roof into a raked shed roof. For the conversation area close to the fireplace, she had kept the ceiling low, creating a cozy hearth-side feeling.

"Where are the bedrooms?" I asked. "Up," said the owners. Up meaning five steps to the next level, where two wood-paneled bedrooms flanked a small bath. An open plan family room looked out through sliding glass doors to a patio. This level was built right into the hillside and created the feeling that you were living right in the woods. The all-purpose room doubled as an office, playroom, laundry, TV, and relaxing room. Even the laundry sink counter could become a bar or an ironing board. A short ladder led up to a small attic built over the laundry counter.

Admittedly, the house was very small, and there was no garage to house the two cars which John and I needed as a working couple. But I liked its location in this unique pocket of Minnetonka woods, yet so close to the city. Because of the warmth and character of this wood-clad house, I felt it was like my own ski chalet—one that only a discerning architect could have designed. No wonder we bought it after only one short visit. Privately I mused that the extra bedroom could become a nursery some day. And it did.

A turmoil of events followed. Soon I found myself divorced, a single parent, hanging onto my career in the ad agency business to keep what was now *my* little house in the woods. Fortunately, I did keep it. It meant so much to me because this is where my only child was born and grew up.

15
Balancing Career
and Motherhood

Now that I was a single-parent working mom, I quickly realized that I was twice as busy as I had been before. My boss agreed with my insistence on shorter hours so that I could pick up Susan at the babysitter's house by five o'clock every night.

That helped a lot and this routine continued for at least a year or more. I still handled my job at the agency just as well, working hard to get everything done, but I missed those special times I could have had with my daughter. I had found a very good sitter who lived right across the highway from us in a house where she handled three or four children every weekday, and Susan seemed happy at Ruthie's house where she could play with other children, but I was still lonesome for her and talked with other women friends about how they handled similar situations.

Some moms cut their jobs down to part-time, others strike a balance such as taking an extra day off every week or working from home when possible. It is always a difficult decision. I much preferred having my child at home in her own environment, where she could play with the little boys next door and she and I could do fun things together. Also, there were some agency projects I arranged to do at home, like writing commercials for Twin City Federal, Dairy Queen or other companies.

I managed to work out a balance for two years until the day came when everything in my world changed. I met Dick Hammel. Once we were married, that brought on another kind of balancing act: child caring, life with a new husband, and freelancing.

16
Meeting My Prince Charming

I continued to work at Colle & McVoy ad agency and noticed how nicely my boss treated me then, even though I announced flatly that I would be coming in later and going home earlier. I had good child care for Susan but began to think that she (and I) would be better off if she had a new adult life partner around. Coincidentally, an architect friend and his wife also understood my situation and arranged a dinner at their lake home. It would be an ideal time for me to meet a new man—also an architect.

I arrived a little early at the Graffunder's lake home and nervously fussed with my hair before their guest arrived. The door opened and my heart skipped a beat when a tall attractive man with a shock of black hair walked in with a smile. Here was a man with great confidence, it showed in the way he moved and carried himself. "Hi," he said. "I'm Dick Hammel." I still remember what I was wearing, my new yellow pant suit and yes, slightly high heels. We sat down together and immediately began talking. We soon discovered that we knew many of the same people and that we loved the lake, Carl's house (an A-frame) and fellow Democrats. After dinner, our host suggested to Dick that he follow me home just to make sure I had a safe trip. That was a sly move because Dick could then see that I lived in an Elizabeth Close-designed house where my little three-year-old daughter was asleep and the babysitter was just leaving. The very next day Dick called and we made arrangements to see mutual friends, the Living-

Dick and I were married in 1970, and enjoyed life with Susan in the Minnetonka woods.

stons, for dinner. We both knew instinctively that we were attracted to one another.

Our romance grew so fast that we could hardly stand to be away from each other. I was convinced that I had never met a finer man than Dick and that my life would be better just for having met him. Within three months, we were engaged; I had learned about his divorce, how his wife was difficult, had a stormy character, and had actually left him and their two children for several months. By the time I met Dick, he was living alone and his two offspring, Anne and Stephen, now young adults, were also on their own.

Meanwhile, it was also important to Dick that I meet his favorite brother, Rusty, and his wife, Audrey. We immediately hit it off, with Rusty declaring that I reminded him of Carol Burnett.

The Hammels were what I'd call "top dog" in Owatonna, Minnesota, where Dick's father had been the mayor and founded a concrete business. His mother taught piano lessons for years, and was the absolute matriarch of the family which included Dick's three brothers, well known businessmen, their wives and offspring. I was happy to realize that Susan and I would soon become part of a large family based in Owatonna at first, then scattered to the winds but still close. The Jones family, on the other hand, had suffered the early loss of my brother, Tom, leaving his widow and three sons.

Our wedding took place on July 18, 1970, in Bar Harbor, Maine. Dick had gotten to know Rev. Arthur Foote, who officiated, when he served as minister of Unity Unitarian Church in St. Paul, which Dick had remodeled after a fire. Reverend Foote later retired to his ancestral home in Southwest Harbor, Maine, and Dick contacted him about holding our ceremony out in Maine.

The wedding took place on a tip of land overlooking the Atlantic, with Rusty and Audrey Hammel as our witnesses. A few other guests came from Minnesota and elsewhere. A boisterous reception at Axel's Lobster Pond followed, complete with champagne, martinis, and wines.

After a brief weekend that included sailing in Arthur's boat, we returned to Minnesota, but we weren't quite through with the honeymoon. Back home, Dick had planned a spe-

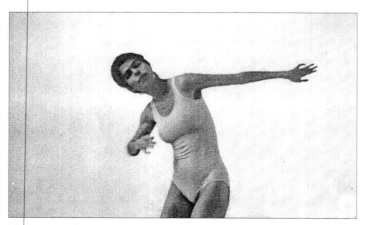

The graceful modern dancer, Anne Hammel, Dick's daughter, who became my second daughter.

cial time for Susan to join us for a sailing trip on Lake of the Woods in northern Minnesota where we stayed at a cabin by the shore. Next day we headed out on the C-boat for a "nice" sailing day. It turned into a hair-raising adventure when a storm suddenly blew in and we flew back toward the cabin with Susan and I clutching each other and hanging out. Later Susan told me she loved that wild ride with the water splashing in her face, while I had held on for dear life. After that, it was a relief to get home and for Dick to get settled with us in the little cedar-clad house in the Big Woods of Minnetonka.

17
Married Life with Dick

After Dick settled comfortably into the Wood Lane house, I was still working and kindergarten had started for Susan. That did it. I quit my full-time job and became a free-lancer. In addition, I realized happily that now I would have time for volunteerism. The Minnetonka Arts Center was the perfect place to begin with a variety of classes for children and adults. First, I signed up Susan for a pottery class which she enjoyed while I joined the Art Center's publicity committee and soon became chair.

Meanwhile, Dick began devising ways he could enlarge the house, originally designed by the esteemed architect Eliza-

The new kitchen of our house in the woods

beth Close. Earlier, he had worked with her husband, Winston Close, at the University. Both Closes were original Bauhaus planners. Every evening Dick sat at his drawing board drawing plans.

The first project was to design a badly needed garage large enough to hold two cars and a boat. It featured a modern slanting roof and sat easily at the end of our wide driveway. Next he created a whole new kitchen and a remodeled entry. I was thrilled with the results. My new all-white galley kitchen had all new appliances, a built-in laundry, and a breakfast counter with a narrow slat window facing the front walkway. For color I placed little red pots filled with red begonias on the counter.

Dick and me with Susan at home.

A larger window overlooked the marsh. The space was so functional, I could do the laundry, cook, make phone calls, and oversee the front yard to check on kids. In Dick's remodel of the small front entry he supported the coat closet with a birch tree trunk that he found in the neighborhood.

Those were the smaller projects. Dick's final objective involved designing a new addition that produced a new master bedroom, bath and dressing room, plus a another cedar-lined room which we called the music room. Both were beautiful simple rooms with large windows bringing the outdoors in. A new cedar deck connected the addition to the older part of the house. Now it was no longer a Close house, but a Hammel/Close house. Elizabeth and Winston Close came out to see Dick's improvements and highly approved of his modernist designs.

At Christmas, my mother-in-law, Helen, sent me a wonderful surprise check for an upright Yamaha piano. I was thrilled, never having had a piano of my own. It was for Susan's benefit too because her Grandma Helen, a piano teacher in her home town, noticed her granddaughter's interest whenever Susan visited her home in Owatonna, Minnesota. Right away, I sought piano lessons for both of us. My daughter was 7 and she learned the scales easily. I signed up for lessons from Marie Graffunder who taught chords and improvising at the Minnetonka Arts Center. I struggled for years but my daughter wound up playing a major recital for family and friends during her senior year at Wayzata High School, and continued playing at Carleton College. (After Helen Hammel's death, Susan inherited her grand piano which she still uses in her own home.)

Between volunteer activities, I began checking my contacts for writing assignments. These turned into public relations projects which I enjoyed because I was writing about real people instead of commercial products. Don Padilla (Padilla and Speer), my p.r. mentor, returned my first call and asked me to help him on a project that involved raising public awareness of the Lindbergh Fund. This special foundation was created by Anne and Charles Lindbergh in 1977, a half-century after the date of his celebrated flight to Paris. The purpose of the Fund is to promote and support innovative technology in the world of aviation.

My assignment was to create a special event at the State Capitol that would feature the Lindbergh Fund winner. Together, Padilla and I thought of the Willmar, Minnesota, boy who was an astronaut and became famous for stepping outside the spaceship for the first time. At that time, I learned that "Pinky" Nelson was residing in Fargo, North Dakota. He was very willing to come to Saint Paul and speak at the State Capitol. I figured, everyone would be eager to meet a real astronaut. We set the date, then planned a dinner hosted by the Lindbergh Board of Directors. Once the publicity was issued, a crowd of people attended the event held in the Capitol Rotunda. I still remember how impressed I was to meet and hear

Dick and Anne flying kites on the beach in New Jersey

"Pinky" talk about his awesome experience in space—very mindful of Charles Lindbergh's first flight. This brave young man stressed that the space program got under way only because the USA was united in demonstrating the importance of mankind in space, and he had high hopes for further exploration. Everyone was thrilled, including the Lindbergh Board.

There were lots of volunteer jobs in the non-profit world that needed professional help. One that appealed to me was helping the Minnesota Orchestra. Through WAMSO, the women's organization of the orchestra, I served on the board as public affairs director and every year I took members to call on legislators for more funding for the arts community.

In the 80s, I was asked to join the Board of IOCP (Interfaith Outreach & Community Partners) located in Wayzata. This charitable organization helps the surrounding communities in many ways ranging from donating food and clothing to helping with medical problems and finding affordable housing. At one board meeting, I heard that single parent mothers needed new underwear for their children. That rang a bell for me. "How about having an event before Christmas at my house, call it 'Undie Sunday,' and ask invited guests to bring new undies for kids?" Everyone loved the idea. We formed a committee and recruited others to bring food, appetizers, dessert and beverages. A friend played Christmas carols, another decorated the room with holiday lights. Invitations were sent to a wide list of prospects. The event turned into a great party and everyone brought bags of new undies. The next day I filled my car with hosts of undies and delivered them to IOCP. Undie Sunday was such a success that it continued for the next 27 years.

Dick, Susan, and I continued to live happily in our house in the woods for almost 20 years, and Anne Hammel would leave her abode in Manhattan for an annual summer visit with us.

A neighborhood dog adopted us because she loved running around our swamp. She was a sleek Norwegian elkhound with a curly tail named Sukie who soon became our beloved pet, even though she rarely came into the house. Dick designed a doghouse for her on the deck where she slept outside our bedrooms.

We also acquired a trampoline for Susan that was a great attraction for the neighborhood girls. Every Halloween, we invited all the local children to visit after tricks and treats. Then, at the window seat by the fireplace, Dick would tell ghost stories and all the children listened quietly while eating their treats.

We loved our newly expanded house on "golden swamp," as Dick called it. Susan grew up in this modern environment nestled in the Minnetonka woods until graduation from Wayzata High School. Then it was off to Carleton College, leaving a big hole in our household, and two parents lonely but ever-optimistic about the future.

18
Catching the Wind

Dick's favorite pastime ever since boyhood, was sailing, especially racing his own sailboat. In contrast, I was a skier, not a sailor—yet. Not long after we first met, he took me out for a sailboat race on White Bear Lake. We lost. C-boats are tippy, but I managed okay, thereby passing the test. Whew!

As part of our marriage, we agreed to take up each other's sport. Accordingly, we joined the Lake Minnetonka Yacht Club, which provided buoys in Carson's Bay for members. Thus began a historic tradition for our Hammel family.

During those early years, I was slated as Dick's first crew, which meant ducking my head to avoid hitting the boom that held the main sail and leaning out to help balance the boat. The start of the race always made my adrenaline go way up. It is so exciting when all the various fleets of sailboats vie to get the best start when the gun goes off for their particular fleet. Then away you go—fast on a C-scow. One cloudy day, a storm came up so suddenly that the judge signaled "head for home." And away we flew, so fast that as we approached the yacht club island Dick could hardly make the turn and yelled at Susan (then only about 7 or 8) to go forward and grab the bow line. She crawled forward, grabbed the line, then we came about and swiftly landed.

In later years, Susan, then married to a sailor, became highly skilled crewing for the best, and eventually skippering her own Yngling racing sloop.

We were ready to collapse, at least I was, and decided it

(above) Our skipper: Dick loved sailing.
(below) Sailing the Yngling in a very competitive fleet.

was time for Dick to find a new crew member. Fortunately, we knew of a young friend who was a powerful skier. His name was Stuart Hanley and he jumped at the chance to become a sailor. He learned a lot from Dick and eventually bought his own boat.

Later on, the yacht club decided to take on their first keelboats. The Yngling was originally designed in Norway as a small racing sailboat about 20 feet long, using three sails including a spinnaker, and could accommodate a crew of three. Dick decided to buy our own Yngling, knowing it was a safer non-tippy boat and fun for all.

With a sigh of relief, I agreed. So off we went on our first race without any tips for me from my skipper on what I should do as crew. At the first mark, Dick ordered me to go forward, take the jib down, and pull up the spinnaker. This meant stepping out on the fore-deck and precariously trying to balance myself while dealing with this huge new sail. Naturally, I messed up, managing to do a "Chinese jib," wrapping the spinnaker around the mast. At least we didn't tip, but it took Dick some time to untangle the twisted sails and keep going with just the main sail. Another learning experience! Dick continued to race for the next 15 years and even managed to win a couple of races. Once in a while, I

I cruised Lake Minnetonka with the *Blue Note*.

helped crew in the Yngling. Sailing is a great sport requiring certain skills such as the ability to "read" the lake's wind and diagnose the best direction for tacking, navigating around the opposition, and handling the spinnaker swiftly and well.

Eventually, I decided I was better off driving our motorboat.

In fact, I became quite skilled at towing Dick and the Yngling from the buoy out to the clubhouse island and even helped tow in other boats when the winds died and skippers needed help getting back to their moorings. Yes, the *Blue Note*, a used Criss-craft, served me very well over the years.

Meanwhile, the Caribbean was beckoning for Dick and his brother. They left for Saint Thomas in the U.S. Virgin Islands and chartered a yacht for a few trial runs. They loved it, and promptly invited us wives along for a real cruise of several islands. Unfortunately for Audrey Hammel, we encountered heavy winds the first day and as the designated cook, she almost quit on the job. Weather improved and we could safely enjoy another beautiful island luscious with palm trees, flowers, a lovely beach and calm waters. I experienced two more Caribbean trips: one with our whole family and another with good friends. That time, we sailed as far as the Spanish Virgin Islands. Sailing in these waters is the absolute perfect vacation— the scenery is spectacular, the food available at small outdoor cafes is delicious, and the swimming or diving off the boat loads of fun while strains of Caribbean rhythms play on shore.

Returning home to a new residence on Grove Lane, we found living at Lake Minnetonka was wonderful summer and winter. It was fun to watch the seasons change thanks to our glassed-in atrium. In winter we watched for the ice houses to pop up at certain vital fishing spots. In fall everyone came out to move their boats out of the marina. Spring was the happy time when we all moored our boats once again. Summer became racing time with picnics at the yacht club island. I grew to know and love Lake Minnetonka, with its rich history and lore.

19
Canvassing Cathedrals in Italy

One spring day, Dick was packing for a business trip to Malaysia where he and a partner would be interviewed for a big hospital commission. I felt a little distressed that he was going so far away. Then he announced a big surprise. "We will be flying home via Europe, so why don't you and Susan meet me in Milan and then we'll go see more of Italy?" he said, smiling. My distress turned to excitement. I had seen Rome before, but not with an architect, especially MY architect.

We called our travel agent immediately and began planning how to get to Milan on a certain date. The plans worked. It was spring break for Susan, then age 13, so we arrived in Milan late in March 1977. We waited impatiently at the agreed hotel for Dick; when he appeared we had a joyous reunion.

The next morning we set out to visit the famed Milan Cathedral, the Duomo of St. Mary's, which Dick said was the largest Gothic cathedral in the world. Looking up at the massive marble structure with its imposing tall spires punctuating the skyline, Susan immediately cried, "Let's go up on the roof, Dad." We didn't know that we would be climbing up 200 steps, but the view was worth it; we could see all over this large ultra-modern city. The cathedral was breathtaking with its complex design, stained glass windows, and interior details. No wonder it took 600 years to build! We rode the elevator down and then walked to another architectural must: the Galleria Victorio Emmanuele II. Dick explained that this was a forerunner of the modern shopping mall designed in the 19th

Century with a cast iron roof and glass vaulted arches.

After renting a car the next day, our architect, following his own itinerary, drove us to Venice where he wanted to see one of the world's most famous plazas, the Piazza San Marco, and we wanted to ride in a gondola on the Grand Canal. We did both. Who doesn't love Venice! It is so amazing when you arrive to step into a boat (rather than a car) to get to your hotel. For those of us who love water, we were enchanted with this city, taking the colorful water taxis to see the Rialto Bridge, other bridges, St. Mark's Basilica, the Doge's Palace, and the Gallerie dell'Academia. I was determined to visit this museum as I had just completed a course on Italian painters at the Minnetonka Arts Center. I wandered up and down, oo-ing and ah-ing the work of Renaissance painters such as Titian, Giotto, Bellini, Leonardo da Vinci, and others.

Finally Susan announced, "We have had enough bambinos, Mom, we're leaving." She and Dick promptly left without a backward glance. Later, we met at Harry's Bar, the so-called "American bar" in this fabulous city.

Dick was now anxious to drive to Cararra, located at the tip of Tuscany, home of the great marble quarries used by architects and builders all over the world. Even our own Minnesota State Capitol is sheathed in it The marble, all white and blue grey, lies on a mountainside by a river in northern Italy.

En route to Florence, we stopped at Pisa to visit the Leaning Tower. This 14th Century architectural cylinder is built of striped white marble and at first glimpse seems to tilt to the right. Of course our 13-year-old had to climb to the top. But not alone; she insisted, we had to climb up there too. Several other fearless tourists followed and we all had a chuckle looking down on pedestrians below. Luckily, the year was 1977, long before the government clamped down for safety reasons. I wonder how far it leans now?

The Duomo in Florence

For our next short stop, we wandered into the village of San Gimignano. Attracted by its skyline of towers, Dick stopped to take a look around and found it so enchanting, we stayed overnight. This walled hill town is famous for its 14 medieval towers that make it a unique place to visit. Dick was so intrigued as we walked around the towers that he took out his art pad and began sketching. All the towers are built of stone similar to other nearby towns such as Siena. The San Gimignano towers made such an impression on Dick that he sketched them again on the backsplash of our new buffet in the Wood Lane house.

Our drive continued south to Florence which, as most tourists know, contains many of the most famous gems of Italian art and architecture packed into one city. As we approached we caught a glimpse of the famous red brick Duomo that announces Florence. On arrival, we finally managed to get close to the Dome, one of the Renaissance's great achievements in architecture. Dick was amazed at Brunelleschi's engineering genius to create this egg-shaped hollow dome in the 15th century. Looking up at it, we could see its shape—eight pointed white arch ribs built without scaffolding. These somehow supported the heavy brick of the dome and also the cupola. The façade is decorated in pink, white, and green marble. We were told the best way to see it was to climb to the top, which Susan had already figured out. Because it was a climb of 473 steps along an extremely narrow stairway once used by the workers, Susan was the only one who made it. By climbing, you also get a fantastic view of the impressive Bell Tower by Giotto that flanks the Duomo.

As we walked the streets, the next "must" was the Palazzo Vecchio, Florence's town hall and sometime home of the powerful Medicis, where a copy of the great statue of David by Michelangelo stands at the entrance. After that and more sightseeing, it was time to leave for Rome.

But along the way, we couldn't resist a stop in Assisi, birthplace of Saint Francis, known as the patron saint of animals and the environment. In 1228, after his canonization as a saint, the Basilica of St. Francis was built to honor this humble man, who lived a life of poverty. Even our architect was surprised to find that this cathedral was built low to the ground and sited on a substantial slope in the Umbrian hills. There are two sections, upper and lower, both of Romanesque style. The upper level, of white brick stretching along the embankment, is the brighter section, with a huge rose window and historic frescoes by Giotto, now faded. There is something touching about seeing where St. Francis once lived.

Rome, this majestic city laid out on its seven hills, always remains imposing, historically fascinating, filled with fountains, churches and entertainment. We had such a good time here, after I got over my shock of mistakenly driving down the Piazza Navona. We stayed in a first class smaller hotel near the plaza known for its famous fountain by Bernini.

Our first destination was St. Peter's and the Vatican, which were important for both Susan and me to see as practicing Catholics. The Basilica, surrounded by its own walled city, was built in the 1500's in the Renaissance and Baroque styles. We were standing in a huge crowd all looking equally amazed at the sight of the Pope's home and center of the Roman Catholic Church. Dick admired the geometric lineup of Doric columns in the plaza. Susan, as usual, pointed to the top roofline and guessed that there must be a way to get up there. Sure enough. We discovered a special entrance off to one side where you can take either an elevator or climb all the way. Naturally, our daughter took the steps, close to over 491, we chose taking the elevator partway.) From there we had a breathtaking rooftop view of the mighty city and of Michelangelo's Dome, the Vatican Gardens and papal apartments. Touring the Sistine Chapel with its sublime ceiling, also by Michelangelo, was another highlight.

We found there were many fascinating spots in Rome including the Trevi Fountain and the Spanish Steps, but we really wanted to concentrate on ancient Rome. To see the Colosseum, the guide books say you must walk around the whole thing. So we did. It's enormous but as we walked, Dick noted the different stages of ruin and the affected columns. Finally we entered and stood on restored wooden steps staring at the huge stadium-type arena down below. It made me shudder to think this was a place where gladiators fought and were killed. Near the Colosseum was the Imperial Forums built 19 centuries ago and begun by Julius Caesar. They were in partial ruins so that we tourists stood at a railing and looked down into the ground to see where the center of once powerful Rome once stood. Only a few columns were left standing plus other scattered remains. Still, a walk around ancient Rome was a must for us history fans.

On with the tour. Dick explained we would be heading south towards the city of Sorrento where we would stay overnight before starting the Amalfi Coast. One look at this tiny narrow coastal highway way up over rocky cliffs and I said, "Dick, you drive." I knew what a good driver he was, even with only one good eye. Susan sat in back hardly daring to look over the rocky side, which dropped perhaps 500 feet to the Mediterranean below. We were headed for Ravello.

Visualize the high cliffs, the narrow road, tiny villages clinging to the mountain side, a shining sea. We were thrilled with the scene as we slowly approached Ravello, located above the more touristy town of Positano at the seashore. Friends from Afton, Minnesota, had recommended that we stay at an ancient hostelry, probably a former palace, where its elderly owner presided. Ravello's plaza was deserted that day when he warmly greeted us. I think he expected a much larger family than ours. We were shown to a huge bedroom with an adjoining smaller one for our young daughter. I felt as though we were in another century; all the furnishings were from historic periods. The same applied to the exterior, a low rambling structure perched at the edge of a cliff overlooking the azure sea. The scene must be one of the most romantic anywhere.

At dinner, Dick and our aged host, who turned out to be a delightful Italian who spoke fluent English, discussed World War II and its effect upon the Amalfi villages. Meanwhile, we were served homemade potato chips, and from our seats we could partially see the cooks preparing a seafood dinner. I could tell that Susan was getting a little bored with all this conversation when she spotted a piano in the room. Asking if it would be okay if she played, everyone nodded yes.

As my lovely fair-haired daughter began, she played her favorites—lively American ragtime tunes by Scott Joplin. Her music immediately attracted every staffer to peer over the kitchen door, and they smiled with delight at the Americano's music. It was a scene to remember: my daughter playing American music in an ancient Italian hostelry by the sea.

Of all my European trips, this was my favorite.

20
New Lake House Gleams

If you were to choose the ideal place to live, wouldn't you want a house by a lake? We did. In 1983, we saw a possibility but decided to check out the site first. When Dick and I drove our motorboat into the Wayzata lagoon and viewed the Grove Lane house across the street, we spotted a tall modern house with a wall of windows facing Lake Minnetonka, a gem of a lake with 125 miles of shoreline. "That has got to be ours," we gasped. Another plus for this location: leasing a book slip in the Wayzata lagoon. We promptly called the real estate agent for a tour.

Obviously, the architect liked angles because upon entering, we immediately noted that the main floor was divided into two areas: on the left, the kitchen; on the right, the living room. In the front, the glass façade drew us into a spectacular atrium facing the lake composed of three levels of glass reaching high up to a loft. "Great!" we exclaimed. I was also happy to see that an old chimney held a working fireplace and that there was a glass-flanked corner for dining. Out the front door sat a small triangular-shaped deck and enough room for two chairs, a small table, and a flower pot.

We learned that an old traditional house had once stood here. But architect John Smith, AIA, and his brother Billy, the builder, saw the potential of the hilly site. They began in 1981 and finished in two years with the intent of selling it "on spec." Billy prepared the land, excavating an area for a ground floor to hold the furnace, laundry, storage, and sauna. Another

entry opened to a pathway down to the lake. In total, the two brothers built a three-story wood-shingled house at the corner of Grove Lane.

We eagerly moved into our new lake home in 1984 after selling out previous residence on Wood Lane. Some remodeling was needed: first the approach to the house from the garage, which was built on a higher level. Dick designed a bridge to link the simple two-car garage to the front door. It was a sturdy cedar bridge that curved around the garage and ended with a Hammel touch: a wood wall shaped like a doorway with a window space for hanging plants. Alongside the bridge, a square-shaped planter was dug out ready for me to plant an annual garden.

Indoors, we were thrilled with the solarium, the most dramatic room in the house. It created quite a stir whenever guests arrived. Not many homes have three levels of glass bringing the outdoors in or at night reflecting twinkling lights and the sky overhead. This ultra-modern space became the perfect place for parties, so I initiated an annual "Undie Sunday" event for the benefit of Interfaith Outreach to be held the first Sunday of December. It was so successful that it has continued for 27 years. Peggy Watson always tacked up strings of Christmas lighting over the window frames, creating a spectacular effect.

Other remodeling was fairly simple. The main floor guest room was given more closet space while the ground floor area became a rec room and a place for major storage. For the living room, Dick built a library wall and a beautiful oak buffet holding my special dishes. A new lighting plan brightened the whole room.

The second floor loft became our new office with a long counter on either side, files below, plus a spot for my computer and Dick's drawing board. The room was painted white, accented by red architecture lamps and blue files. The bonus? A magnificent lake view where I continued to work for many years.

I found the sunny kitchen, which had a helpful island, to be a good functional space as is. A partial wall divided the kitchen from the solarium. I enjoyed cooking in this bright space and the oak dining table was just steps away facing the lake.

After Susan experienced the house a few times, she became intrigued too and soon she invited a group of her favorite classmates for a weekend party. The morning after, I remember seeing Carletonians stretched out in their sleeping bags on every deck outside and any floor available inside. Everyone loved our house by the lake.

UNFORTUNATELY, AFTER ONLY two years of enjoying our very special lake home, Dick became ill. His health began to decline in the fall of his 63rd year. He confessed to me that driving home one evening after work, he had to pull off the road because he felt he was suddenly blacking out. This was so disturbing that he called the doctor the next day. The diagnosis was not good: lymphoma on the left side.

Cancer had hit my splendid husband, unexpected because his left eye, effected by a peculiar circulatory system, had always been a severe problem. It was called a hemangioma, and it caused his eye to bulge slightly. Despite that problem, Dick practiced architecture successfully for years with only one good eye.

In the end, that condition plus lymphoma (the same kind that killed Jackie Kennedy) led to Dick's death at the University of Minnesota Hospital on November 18, 1986. His funeral, held at Colonial Church of Edina, was packed with family, friends, and the whole HGA staff, young and old. As I recall, it was his original partner, Curt Green, who gave the eulogy; Arthur Rouner led the service. Curt looked stunned, and expressed the shock of all 200 staff members who regarded Dick as their leader by repeating "Who would have thunk it? Who would have thunk it?" Men and women staffers valued Dick as a friend, and not just as the company leader. Yet leader he was, right up to the end, always looking for their next big project. Everyone knew that he was the one with the innate ability to articulate the next architectural challenge and how his well-qualified staff would solve it. Dick's passing meant the end of an era. I was devastated, but friends and family dropped in easily and often; neighbors were helpful and generous.

While grieving, I continued to love living in our light-filled house and worked hard to maintain it according to Hammel standards. The second floor office was perfect during my writing and publishing years and I managed to fill it up. I also took pride in making improvements. The wood-burning fireplace was the biggest challenge. I replaced it with gas, which required a lot of work beforehand. John Smith, the original architect, advised me on the project. The original stone chimney was crumbling and needed a complete cleaning and the hearth needed to be rebuilt. I found attractive tiles to place over the old sill so that it became a narrow bench for sitting. Result? A tidy new fireplace center that created a cozy spot for winter entertaining.

After my grandchildren were born in the late 90's, I had fun redecorating the guest bedroom on the main floor. That required buying twin beds, colorful quilts, other bedding, and bed lights. I always enjoyed having Caleigh and Danny sleep over when they were growing up and I know they did too.

For thirty years I lived alone in my Lake Minnetonka home, enjoying the light that filled the house, the feeling of living almost outdoors, the ready access to the lake and to "downtown" Wayzata. Mainly, I went back to being my old "career girl" self. During these years I worked happily on the "Legendary" series of coffee table books with my colleague, photographer Karen Melvin. We created three best-selling books: *Legendary Homes of Lake Minnetonka, Legendary Homes of the Minneapolis Lakes, Great Homes of Summit Avenue* and later my own book, *Wild About Architecture.*

To celebrate their completion, Karen's husband, Phil Prowse, invited us to a suburban field where the power parachute ultra light aircraft were parked. "You've got to have a ride and see how I shot those aerials of those great Minnetonka houses," he said. We women watched nervously as one of the little "planes" took off. But when I saw how easily it climbed into the air, I was eager to go up myself. They strapped me in right behind the pilot, and gave me a helmet and ear phones. The pilot revved up the motor and we started roaring across the field. The parachute trailing behind gradually filled with air and suddenly we were lifted into the sky. I felt totally exhilarated. As we approached Lake Minnetonka, the pilot flew low enough so I could get a full view of the Pillsbury House and estate, many other houses, and the Caribbean Tonka Bay restaurant. I even got a whiff of the burgers cooking on the grill. Never before had I appreciated the length and breadth of "our lake." The ride lasted only about 10 or 15 minutes but it was unforgettable. It remains in my memory as another "career girl" life adventure, but perhaps not my last. Who knows?

21
Becoming an Author

After losing Dick, I kept busy for about a year going to grief groups, but I was still despondent. Like any "career girl," I knew that a new assignment would help restore me so I called HGA and asked, "Would you like me to write something about Dick's history with the firm?" The answer was an unqualified "yes" from Dick's partners. In fact, they said that a complete history of the company was needed because they were approaching their 35th anniversary.

Wow! No more crying in the closet, no more grief groups, I was facing a major challenging assignment. First, however, I had to figure out how to deal with 50 vice presidents. I turned to Carol Pine, an expert on writing company histories, who suggested that I appoint a committee to help me expedite the job.

I immediately asked Curt Green, Dick's first partner, to be chairman, and together we named three architects, two engineers, one interior designer and one from landscape. For my first interview, I chose structural engineer, Yanak Shagalov, who taught me how vital the structural team was to the initial design of a building. As I continued the interviews from various disciplines, I realized more and more how much I was learning about the language of architecture.

During that year of interviewing and writing, I worked closely with the firm's public relations department. *From Bauhaus to Bowties* was finally published in late 1989 and sent to all libraries in 1990. This was my first book.

An even bigger event followed. Susan graduated from Harvard's Kennedy School of Government in June, 1990, with a master's degree in public policy. Several friends joined me for the ceremony: Susan's finance Tom Joyce, his mother Nancy Joyce, my cousin Paul Bischoff, Susan's college roommate, Laura Day, and my pal, Katie Berg. A Harvard graduation is a thrill to see, what with all the pomp and circumstance, the colorful robes worn by the leading faculty, the band playing, and the scene in the huge courtyard. The speaker was U.S. Secretary of Defense Colin Powell.

Afterwards, the Kennedy School had its own ceremony, and as Susan marched by, we all wildly applauded. She was again at the top of her class and I was so proud. After that, Susan returned to New York to join the Federal Reserve Bank of New York, and we all went back home.

By then I was officially an architectural journalist but where could I find an editor? The *Minneapolis Star Tribune* and *Pioneer Press* already had architectural critics so I decided my one chance might be *Skyway News*. The editor, Jodie Ahern, liked the way I talked so passionately about architecture that she gave me a column which I promptly named "Changing Skyscapes." Soon I was off on my new career in what was then a man's world with the exception of a few talented women architects such as Joan Soranno, Julie Snow, and Rosemary McMonigal. After about a year of writing about new towers, adaptive reuse, and how the Twin Cities was changing with the times, the editor of *Architecture Minnesota* called suggesting that I write short news pieces for the magazine. I was delighted. The timing was right because *Skyway News* was under new ownership and I missed the Bakers trendy style of the paper. For the next few years I interviewed a high percentage of the Minnesota AIA architects. They were a great bunch and told me some fantastic stories.

One of my favorites came from Tom Meyer of Meyer, Scherer & Rockcastle architects. When the Washburn A Mill suddenly caught fire in 1991, the Minnesota Historical Society's chief, Nina Archibald, intervened to save the concrete shell of the burned-out structure. Tom Meyer, who had admired the Mill during his U of M student days, (even sleeping down there at times), came up with a great idea. Why not build a new office tower within part of the burned-out site, saving the shell for future events. Result? A new office tower and a new Mill City Museum emerged and became a huge tourist attraction for the city, complete with a flour tower elevator taking families up to the top and MS&R's shiny new offices overlooking the river.

Meanwhile, an even more important event was taking place in my personal life. Susan's first child was born April 1, 1997, a baby girl who was given an Irish name, Caleigh. It was such a precious moment to coddle my first grandchild in my arms. Two years later, my daughter was blessed with a son named, Danny on Nov. 22,1998. I was thrilled to have two lively grandchildren to keep

me busy. In between assignments, I walked them around the neighborhood in their strollers and helped out whenever Susan needed a babysitter. It seemed like a natural part of a career girl's life to have a proud new title, "Grams."

Next, a new business opportunity came along, though unexpected. The College of Architecture had a new dean, Thomas Fisher, former editor of *Progressive Architecture* magazine in

New York. When we met for the first time I explained that I tried to sell architectural stories. He sympathized, and suggested that I should call on *Architecture Record* in New York. Because Anne Hammel, my step daughter, lived there, I usually flew there once a year, and on my next trip, as advised, I made an appointment to see the managing editor, Cliff Pearson. Nervous and worrying—"Why should a big-time editor want to see an unknown Midwest writer like me"—I approached their offices and was ushered in right away. The moment I gave my name Pearson knew about the firm. Then I relaxed and he asked me a lot of questions about Minnesota architects and their work. Next he introduced me to the executive editor, Bob Ivy. I was warmly received by this southern-gentleman-type man who was very receptive. I walked out of *Architectural Record* with three or four assignments, mostly the short newsy stuff. At first, I worked for them with news stories, but later they gave me features based on my queries. It took 50 years, but I finally made it in New York!

The best of my stories was the one about the restoration of Dubrovnik, jewel of the Mediterranean, which had been damaged during the Bosnian War. The year was 2000 and Carol Pine, our sailing mentor, had just sailed the Adriatic the year before and written a story about the Croatian Islands for *Sailing Magazine*. When she asked if our sailing group would like to go in 2001, six of us (mostly blondes) signed on immediately. Realizing the possibilities of a story, I called on the local Croatian consulate and luckily met a young Croatian native whose father had actually led the construction crew for the renewal of Dubrovnik.

Talk about timing! I now had a name, phone number, and address in Dubrovnik for an *Architectural Record* feature story. I got the assignment before we left. And thanks to our skipper Carol Pine and a good seven-women crew, we included stops

Celebrating my 80th birthday with my two daughters, Anne and Susan, in Orchestra Hall.

at five fantastic islands en route and still arrived in Dubrovnik in time for the interview.

After that exciting trip sailing down the Adriatic for an interview where I had been treated like a genuine foreign correspondent, my mood was high when I came home to write the story. It appeared in the October 2001 issue of *Architectural Record* magazine almost exactly as I had written it, accompanied by photographs by Ann Fisher, a member of our sailing crew. How could I top this, I thought. After that experience, I attended many architecture lectures, studied various books, attended two national AIA conventions and basically built my knowledge of architecture.

From then on, I proudly carried an i.d. showing my name, "architectural journalist," but privately my best title was "Grams."

22
Twin Cities Architecture, Some "Wows"

For the next two years, Twin Cities architecture became my main subject, with one focus being the major differences between the two cities. After years of reporting and leading tour groups through many different places of interest, I've tried to decide which sites are my favorite. Here's a quick summary beginning with my home town, Saint Paul.

The State Capitol comes first. Designed by Cass Gilbert more than a hundred years ago and beautifully restored by HGA to its original glory in 2017, this work of classical architecture moves me more any other Minnesota building possibly can. I remember when a high school friend and I managed to get tickets for the House balcony and sat in sheer awe of the place. Many years later, in 1988, I was appointed to the Capitol Area Architectural and Planning Board commissioned by Governor Rudy Perpich. For six years, I happily entered the stately building for our meetings. Our job was to oversee the Capitol area's existing, new or remodeled architecture and make sure that new designs fit the existing sites, including the mall. Years passed and the Capitol Mall kept changing and adding monuments, I thought a few too many.

Early in 2017, I was fortunate to join a special group tour of the restored Capitol led by Virginia Lackovic and two other top women architects of HGA who managed the design team for this huge restoration project. As we walked and walked

Rice Park in downtown St. Paul

through the huge space, we were overwhelmed by the intricate work done by the craftsmen and women restoring the marble, the dome, the golden horses, the Supreme Court, the artwork especially, and everything down to the tiniest detail in the Governor's reception room.

My other favorite Saint Paul places include: the City Hall with its magical War Memorial Hall of black onyx housing the 36-foot-tall Indian sculpture of the Vision for Peace by sculptor Carl Milles; the former art deco Women's City Club, now offices; the University Club, once a Fitzgerald hangout, a bit tired but still swanky, designed by Reed & Stem in 1913; and especially Rice Park, surrounded by four different eras of architecture: the Landmark Center, the Ordway Center for the Performing Arts, the George Latimer Central Library, and the Saint Paul Hotel.

Lastly, the Minnesota History Center, a monumental building of classical ambiance, designed by Bruce Abrahamson and his HGA team and completed in 1993.

In Minneapolis, I am over the top in praise for Target Field, the Minnesota Twins Ball Park. Why? I love the views of our city from this wide open semi-circular stadium. There's no roof, but a large canopy for shelter, eating, and drinking. It's built of Minnesota Kasota stone and beautifully reflects our state as it curves around the large site located in the historic warehouse district. The architects, Populous of Kansas City, worked closely with locally-based Mortensen Construction and HGA on the construction site to make sure this ultra modern stadium is well-integrated with the city. Bill Blanski of my husband's firm said the main entrance was their particular concern. They designed it as though the city flows right into the ballpark.

My other Minneapolis favorites include two towers: The IDS, designed by Philip Johnson and John Burgee, NYC, 57 stories of offices and retail; it is slim and elegant as though poised to take over the city. I always love walking through the amazing Crystal Court, still the crossroads of downtown. The other tower, ING, originally the Northwestern National Life Insurance building, was designed by Japanese architect Minoru Yamaski, who also designed the World Trade Center in New York. Note the ultra-slim columns flanking the street.

Other modernist buildings that are special include the Minneapolis Central Library, which occupies a block on

Target Field, the Minnesota Twins ball park

Cesar Pelli's library in downtown Minneapolis

Nicollet Mall. The four-story building, designed by Cesar Pelli, has a dashing interior with a handsome artistic floor in the atrium. On the second floor is the Special Collections room set aside for researching area house histories. I have spent many hours doing research there.

In the Mill District, James Dayton designed a contemporary six-story cube-like building as the new home for MacPhail Center for Music. It's a marvel of state-of-the art space for the study of music. Dayton also included a performing arts auditorium with superb acoustics.

My other architectural pursuits were strictly voluntary. In the late 90s, a friend from KUOM days called asking if I could lead an architectural class for ELI, the Elder Learning Institute, a new program for seniors based at the University of Minnesota. I reminded him that I was not an architect but that I could probably set up such a class asking various architects to do the lectures. Steve promptly scheduled the class to begin that fall. For my first class, I called Ralph Rapson, prestigious dean of the U of M's School of Architecture.

The class filled immediately and Ralph, sensing that seniors were very interested, talked about why architecture is so vital to our communities. After that we were on a roll. I began planning the course ranging from art facilities to churches to corporations to retail shops to residential. It was a major job, and I needed help in calling the various architects I had chosen. Virginia Sweatt became my great helper, calling these talented fellows and asking them in her charming way to give us their volunteer time. Ginny and I carried on for 11 years until the time came when ELI became the Oscher Lifelong Learning Institute or Olli.

I especially liked James Dayton's lecture on modernism, the history of which he learned from Frank Gehry when Jim was beginning his career. Gehry and his staff work mainly with models of all shapes and sizes before deciding on solutions for their daring projects.

Having been married to a modernist architect, I feel like one too. I admire the early lessons of modern architecture: simplicity, openness, and design that fits the site. Obviously being involved in architecture has been the highlight of my long career.

The new McPhail Center

The new Bell Museum. [photo by Corey Gaffer]

In 2018, a new architectural icon was built in St. Paul, the Bell Museum of Natural History, designed by the Minneapolis office of Perkins & Will. It is located on the edge of the University of Minnesota's St. Paul campus. Its rectangular form of local granite, white pine, glass, and steel sweeps across the landscape as though compelling the public to enter. A massive entry faces an imposing stairway leading up to a huge, life-size model of a pre-historic mastodon resembling the creatures that once ventured across Minnesota. The building is equally large at 90,000 square feet allowing the public ample space to see the newly restored dioramas and Minnesota's other native inhabitants. Visitors can also step outside on a large deck to admire the landscaping, the green roof and the architect's use of granite blocks. Inside, a digital state-of-the-art planetarium is available for groups of all ages.

Indeed, the Twin Cities can boast of many outstanding works of architecture, both private and public, as visitors have learned. We may be known as "flyover land," but when it comes to architecture, our cultural attractions, international companies, and landscape dotted with lakes, we know we have the best in our twin towns here on the Mississippi.

23
House Histories Live in Legendary Series

While attending an architect's open house in 2003, I met a photographer who also lived on Lake Minnetonka. Her house was on the upper lake while mine overlooked Wayzata Bay on the lower lake. As we chatted, I mentioned that I had always wanted to do a story about Minnetonka's boathouses. We then decided to do this together via my boat or hers. That decision was the beginning of a long collegial partnership between photographer Karen Melvin and writer Bette Hammel.

After we finished the boathouse story in photographs and text, we promptly sold it to *Minneapolis/St. Paul* magazine in 2005. Triumphantly, we decided we had learned so much about the homes above the boat houses that we should focus on them and do a book about these fascinating works of architecture.

We began by selecting the houses from our boats. We chose a variety, not just the grandest homes but some more affordable, smaller versions in a variety of architectural styles. The next step was to get permission from the home owners for interviews and photography, mainly of their public spaces inside and out.

After my first interview, Karen would then make a date for photography. The homeowners were all very cooperative and seemed to enjoy the process as long as we were not invading their private spaces. It was a long process that occupied the summers of 2008 and 2009, and during that time I learned a lot about residential architectural styles ranging from Classic and Colonial Revival to Art Deco, Tudor and Modern. Two of my favorite houses were the grand Pillsbury estate and a small A-frame owned and designed by Carl Graffunder on Hardscrabble Point, where years ago I had been introduced to my dear husband Dick.

With the Minnesota Historical Society Press as our publisher, we had to raise the money to have the book printed in China. Full color printing of a large coffee-table size book is very expensive. I spent many hours fund-raising, which was successful since this was a non-profit endeavor. *Legendary Homes of Lake Minnetonka* was finally published in 2010 and has continued to sell ever since.

Our next book, *Legendary Homes of the Minneapolis Lakes*, has remained my favorite because it reveals an urban landscape, and there are a greater variety of architectural styles in the Minneapolis Chain of Lakes area than on Lake Minnetonka.

Among the houses we chose for the book was the oldest Lake of the Isles residence, which had been painfully restored by its owner, Katherine Chrisman, who suffered an early death.

The restored house, a Queen Ann Victorian beauty, was definitely on our radar but we could never reach the owner, Josh Hartnet, a local celebrity who always seemed to be in Hollywood and never home. One day, Karen suddenly spotted the "star" walking down the street near his home. She grabbed our Minnetonka book and rushed after him hoping to show him an example of our work. When she reached him, he showed no interest and walked away. We were crushed. This was our one disappointment in the Lake of the Isles neighborhood.

Despite that failure, we scored a major hit for the book when the prominent owner of a new contemporary house, Bill Pohlad, allowed us to enter his home. We expected to see some impressive artwork in this glass-enclosed space, but to our amazement, instead of a painting, an actual Formula I race car was hanging like a sculpture on the gold Venetian plaster living room wall. It was such a bold dramatic piece, it "blew us away." Talk about living art! This was obviously an expression of the owner's lifestyle; he was already an award-winning filmmaker.

The second book was published by the Minnesota Historical Society in 2012, and yes, it was fun writing about the Chain of Lakes and the residents, too.

The third book, of which I was only one of four writers, *Great Houses of Summit Avenue*, was issued in 2013 and published by Karen Melvin, now established as an independent publisher of Big Picture Press. As such, she wanted to get the book out in one year. Result? Four writers were needed. I was happy that my assignments included the historic brownstone townhouse where F. Scott Fitzgerald had lived briefly. I always loved his books and admired his writing, so I entered the house with considerable interest.

Current owners, the Jones family, were happy to show me where Scott's room had been, and especially the small stone balcony where he could step outside and have a "smoke." This was the spot where he revised *This Side of Paradise* for publication by Scribner in 1923. The book not only made him famous as a new writer of the jazz age, it brought him enough money to marry his beloved Zelda. The so-called writing room is just an ordinary room sparsely furnished to remind fans of where the writer once holed up and called his parents for snacks on a small speaking tube on the wall.

Following publication of the coffee table books, I wanted

to do my own "little" book of pocket size. For the text, I selected some of my favorite articles published in various architecture magazines over the years. Many stories I rewrote to bring them more up to date. Another section I saved for "hero architects," big names such as Cesar Pelli and Frank Gehry. The final chapter told of various favorite cities such as Vancouver, Chicago, and of course, my home town, Saint Paul. Photo illustrations were chosen by Karen from stock, or per-

sonal travel photos of our own. One of the last chapters was my favorite, relating the wonders of Croatia during our sailing trip to Dubrovnik in 2001.

The 218-page *Wild About Architecture* book was issued in 2016.

24
Croatia: Six Blondes
Sail the Islands

"You are invited to join me on a bareboat yachting cruise through the beautiful islands of Croatia via the Adriatic as far as Dubrovnik," wrote Carol Pine in a note to a small group of women sailors in 2000. Having seen photos of her experiences sailing there, six of us immediately jumped at the chance.

As the eldest member of the group, I accepted with some concern that the only thing I remembered about sailing was how to handle the jib—

So I signed up. Carol was an experienced skipper with the Wayzata Yacht Club of Lake Minnetonka. She had raced in three international Rolex Keelboat regattas for women only, and sailed in international waters with all-female crews. The agreement meant we would share renting a 45-foot yacht for one week from the marina of Trogir, Croatia. Six of us predominately blonde Minnesotans agreed to help crew and began planning for the May 2001 trip.

Once we had all assembled in Croatia, I began to realize this was going to be a major undertaking. What did I really know about how to help crew a big yacht headed for the Mediterranean! Gulp. My past experience was only in the Caribbean when my husband was the captain and navigator.

Very quickly our skipper swung us into action and soon we had completed packing all supplies and gear into the boat, selected our bunks and were ready for morning departure. Meanwhile, we decided to investigate the town of Trogir and find a restaurant for dinner. Our guidebook described the walled town, with early 13th and 15th century buildings, which I was eager to see. We began a leisurely walk past Romanesque and Renaissance architecture including a three-naved Venetian cathedral of impressive proportions. As we wandered through the ancient streets, we spotted a lovely outdoor garden space that seemed to be a small restaurant. No one was around but we walked in anyway. Suddenly an attractive young woman of college age appeared and asked in perfect English, "Would you like to have lunch? Lamb is on the menu." We accepted and then she disappeared. It turned out that she was part of a family operation next door. The lunch she served was delicious, including excellent Croatian wine. We enjoyed her so much that we invited her back to our boat to tell us more about her country. Croatia had just become an independent nation in 1991. She was still furious with the Serbs in the recent Bosnian war and was personally struggling to finish college. Mainly, she was very proud of the art and architecture that had made Trogir a World Heritage Site in 1997.

The next morning we raised the sails, excitedly took our places, and set off for the small island of Hvar. As we approached the island, the lovely scent of lavender wafted in our direction and we could see an entire mountainside filled with lavender. Hvar was a charming place to anchor. We began our entrance into the harbor and headed for a wide long dock where children were gleefully jumping into the water. The harbor master stood frowning when he discerned that we were an all-female crew, but brightened up on spotting the American flag flying on our boat. Pam Nicols, Carol's first mate, masterfully guided our yacht into a slip, maneuvering a perfect Mediterranean stern-to-tie landing with Carol directing and our crew assisting. It was great fun exploring the village, walking the marble streets, stopping at the little shops and enjoying lunch in the town square. What looks like marble, I soon learned, was the wonderful pale-colored limestone used everywhere along the Dalmatian coast.

It didn't take long to find another anchorage for the next night with captain Carol and navigator Mary directing.. Carol had learned that when the Soviets controlled the region in the 80s, they built many substantial marinas, mostly of utilitarian concrete, but very functional. It was easy to anchor in this efficient harbor, where showers and toilet facilities were nearby, also a small restaurant where we enjoyed another tempting Croatian dinner at very reasonable prices.

Learning how to sleep aboard a yacht accommodating six women was the next major adjustment, but I made it, slowly relaxing as the boat rocked gently through the night. Our destinations were all carefully planned in advance to make sure we reached the major goal, Dubrovnik, in time for my interview with the city's rehabilitation contractor.

As our voyage continued, I marveled at the architecture of these various islands, which ranged from medieval to Romanesque to modern touches. Korcula, for example, with its peninsula jutting into the sea, sported a tall rounded medieval tower typical of an old 15th century Dalmatian coast town. It is said that this is the place where Marco Polo had stayed, and I could just visualize the solitary leader arriving in this city for rest on his long journey. Talk about history! We were in it here. Walking through the town, we came to remnants of another walled city, and then a more modern public square where Croatians were enjoying their coffee, shopping, or playing with their children. Korcula was a large island with many vineyards, olive groves and figs growing. Everyone seemed pleased to see us Americans.

We knew that Croatia had once been a part of Yugoslavia and that Tito had been the once-powerful leader. Hearing that the island of Vis was the place to see his now defunct headquarters, we wanted to see it. It was too late for exploring, and not finding a slip there we anchored at a safe distance from a tall concrete wharf. Unfortunately a strong wind came up and we could not stop the boat from constantly swaying and nearing the dock. Despite our numerous boat fenders, the situation led to a sleepless night. In the morning, locals directed us to a trail up the mountainside eventually leading to a cave which Tito and his partisans used for their military base. Another bit of history we chalked off from our list.

As we were getting close to Dubrovnik, Carol spotted an inlet with what appeared to be a tiny resort with a small beach and decided it might be a good anchorage. Just as we headed into the harbor, a young man came running out. When he spotted our American flag and then the all-female crew, he shouted, "Americans! Women!!!" He was so excited, he jumped up and down and rushed to help us land. We were delighted to see his exuberance, and I immediately changed into my bathing suit to swim for the first time on the trip. It was a rocky little beach but I enjoyed it. Meanwhile, when our young host met our pretty blonde captain, I think he fell in love at first sight. From then on, we were treated royally inside and out of his beachside café. We stayed up late and then had a very good night's rest.

Dubrovnik was close by and we sailed into that harbor with much excitement right at breakfast time on board and in plenty of time for my meeting with the contractor. My homework at home was about to pay off. During the Bosnian War, the Serbs had gunned the town destroying many of the original tiles from the roofs of this historic walled city.

As I mentioned in a previous chapter, I knew this would

make a great story for *Architectural Record* magazine and had already gotten the assignment. One of our crew members was my "official" photographer. We called a cab and off we went for my interview with the contractor who had supervised the tile rehabilitation. He could not speak English, but he had a translator there and I began my questions. They treated me like a foreign correspondent and even gave me another man to interview down in the city's offices where I learned the rest of the rehabilitation story, in English this time.

Stepping through the ancient gates of the city, we found that we could easily walk on the walls that surround the whole place and drink in the marvelous views of the Mediterranean. No wonder that all the travel magazines call Dubrovnik "the pearl of the Adriatic." The shops were down the steps and like any tourist, we just had to explore them and find trinkets to take home. After such an exciting day, followed by another sumptuous Croatian dinner overlooking the sea, we headed back to the boat for a much-needed rest.

The next morning, our skipper called the crew into action and as we slowly cruised away from the harbor, Carol suddenly announced, "Bette, this looks like a good place for your swim here. Get your suit on. "In minutes, I was ready, and jumped in with promises from everyone to go slowly. The water was so invigorating, I felt happy to be swimming again, yet as I began with the crawl I could see that the boat was getting well ahead of me. I had hit a current and it was holding me back. "Yikes!" I yelled. "I need help, come back!" Carol had already turned the boat around, the boat ladder had been secured, and members of the crew were ready to throw me a line. Thus ended my big adventure in Dubrovnik. I had completed another career girl's assignment, and there were a lot more beautiful Croatian islands to see on our way back up the Adriatic to our home port.

Chapter 25
Capers with Grandchildren

Beginning with the 21st century, I found that having two bubbly young grandchildren was the most fun yet. There was nothing in my career that had prepared me for the experience of becoming a grandmother. I was thrilled, also determined to achieve a new learning curve.

At first, Susan was working and really needed me. I could easily put aside a freelance assignment to help with baby-sitting. Those were the cuddling years when both Caleigh and Danny were wee toddlers knocking over blocks, playing with the same toys over and over, asking me to read stories and listening to Mr. Rogers. On many days, I took them for rides in their strollers up and down the leafy Highland Park streets, stopping for treats or petting the neighbors' dogs. But wait, they grow so fast. A few years later, my kids could walk and talk, run, jump, climb, swing, splash, and gobble up ice cream.

Caleigh, the elder, loved swinging and climbing all over the neighbors playset. Danny, almost two years younger, liked nothing better than throwing balls, any kind of balls, and he quickly learned to catch them too. During those years when my daughter and her husband lived in St.Paul, I learned where the best playgrounds were located and off we would go via strollers.

One playground outside Expo Elementary was just enormous, with all kinds of planks, ladders, steps, and hiding places. In winter, I would take them over to the Highland Park library, which had easy hills where they learned to slide and have fun playing in the snow.

Danny and Caleigh Joyce, ages four and five swinging at the nearest playground.

Then came the time when my family left their cozy St. Paul home and headed for Reston, Virginia, where Susan's husband had landed a very good job. It was a sad day for me thinking I would now lose my little best friends who called me "Grams."

It wasn't long, however, before Susan invited me to come visit, stay for the holidays, and see Reston, known nationally as one of America's best planned communities. "Also," she said, "the children are anxious to see you." I couldn't wait, of course; freelancing could be put on hold. (By then, I was writing for *Architecture Minnesota* magazine.)

Reston took me by surprise. I recalled Dick talking about such a place. In a planned community like Reston, homes are built into the woods and 50 miles of paved trails connect homes with neighboring schools and commercial corridors. The actual business and city center for Reston was strictly confined to an area up the hills and well designed with shops, offices, and restaurants. I was impressed to see a skating rink in the center of town. With rental equipment handy, I managed to get Caleigh out on the rink, both of us wobbling at first, but somehow we skated. Danny wanted no part of this activity, preferring his beloved baseball.

It didn't take long to get reacquainted with Caleigh and Danny, now in elementary school. In fact, I would often take the trail leading to their school, meet them halfway, and walk home with them. Through my now regular visits (four times a year), I just naturally became part of their lives, walking to the nearby park, for example, located up a big hill shaped like a long green space interspersed with playground, basketball court and a small ballfield. Other times, their play centered around their home's steep drive-way. It was concrete, making a natural place to throw balls down the incline, catch them at the bottom, then run back up. (I did not run up or down.) Another favorite place to visit close by was an architectural landmark: a large plaza of early modernist design featuring a U-shaped open space enclosed with residential units above and retail below. The plaza overlooked

Before I knew it, my grandkids grew into teenagers. Danny, not yet into his growth spurt.

a man-made lake that came right up to the plaza, complete with boat rental and shore lined with attractive townhomes. Robert Simon, who had planned this area, was known far and wide as a gifted city planner.

Reston was very close to Washington D.C. This was a big attraction for me—a chance to really see the city. On days when Susan was working in her home office, I would take the metro into D.C. and start making the rounds on the Smithsonian Mall. I loved the American History museum the best and made sure we brought the children there. Over the holidays Susan would drive us into the city and we agreed that

our nation's capitol is the best looking city in America. I'll never forget visiting at beautiful cherry blossom time, and my grandchildren started running down the street heading for the Lincoln Memorial while their mom cautioned them at stop signs. At Lincoln's monument we took lots of pictures of Danny and Caleigh stopping in awe when close up to Lincoln, then bursting with energy as they ran down the steps, ready to see the next one—the Jefferson Memorial. It was an exhausting day for me but I made it.

Some highlights of other visits include touring the new American Indian Museum with my grandkids, who especially loved climbing over parts of the exterior walls built of Minnesota Kasota stone; and visiting the Newseum, especially appealing to me because it followed the history of broadcasting and what a broadcast studio looked like. Both kids enjoyed sitting in the studio and pretending they were on TV.

My family's next move was to Chicago where Tom had landed another big job. They settled in Hinsdale, a classy suburb known for its beautiful homes and easily accessible by train to the city. By this time, my grandchildren were now in middle school, and they were very busy with after-school activities. But we still had good times together at the local swimming pool, or visiting the shops in Hinsdale, and occasionally traveling into the city to see some of the architectural wonders of Chicago. The huge new Millennium Park designed by Frank Gehry wowed us all. Danny and Caleigh especially loved splashing in the reflecting pool of the Crown Fountain where they laughed as the funny face sculpture on the tower squirted water on them.

It was important to keep in touch with my grandchildren as they grew, continuing the tradition I had with Susan, visiting her wherever she roamed.

When birthdays or holidays drew near, it was easy for me to fly and Susan would meet me at the airport or take the Burlington Northern train offering a scenic ride out of St. Paul, and there was always the bus. From Chicago's loop, it was a quick ride to Hinsdale.

Three years later, much to my joy, Susan brought her children home to Minnesota and found a house near the shores of Lake Minnetonka where she could go sailing again

Caleigh Joyce, 21, at home.

just as she once did with Dick. Her marriage had ended, but she was happily settled in Minnesota again. Close by, she enrolled in the Minnetonka Yacht Club's sailing school and there met an outdoor lover like herself. It wasn't long before she and

Dan Broberg were married and became a combined family with the addition of Dan's two sons.

It was an adjustment for both my grandkids to start over again in new schools. But they are bright children, and I was proud to see them graduate very successfully from Min-

With Danny, now at 6 feet.

netonka High School. I was happy for Caleigh who had proved to be a workaholic, achieved a black belt in the martial arts, and earned a Presidential Service medal for her volunteer work with children that launched a passion for social justice. She is now studying at St. Mary's University, California. And I was tickled for Danny who not only continued to play basketball and base-

ball, but also performed with the school orchestra as a bass player for four years, then won a statewide competition in DECA, an entrepreneurship program, competing internationally and traveling to Spain. When it was time for college, I was happy that he selected my alma mater, the University of Minnesota, and entered the Carlson School of Business.

At some point over the years, Harry Potter entered the scene and both Caleigh and Danny became instant fans. Caleigh, who has read all the Potter books many times over, has tried very hard to turn me into a long lasting fan too. I haven't kept up, I'll admit. But now I think I'm ready to hop on the Hogwarts Express and head for Hogwarts School. After all, we are still ready for more learning even at 93, and I can see that joining the world of magic and mystery could maybe, just maybe, turn me into a mystery writer—in case I need another career.

My grandchildren are now both away in college—Caleigh in California, Danny living on campus at the U of M. Now I can only watch from afar, but I know for sure that they will do well. As I look to the future, I hope they will continue to be my best friends as well their proud grandmother.

Reflections

Now in my nineties, my "career" girl instinct still prevails. And yes, I have lost many dear friends and family over these years including my parents, my brother, Tom, and my husband, Dick. My spiritual life has supported me through these trying times. Like many of us, I've found it's a pleasure to have grandchildren. My two, Caleigh and Danny, are away at college but I can count on them for their caring and friendship.

Their mom, my daughter, Susan, does more for me than I can count. She is the keystone in my life.

As for my "career," my philosophy can be summed up by what a sailing friend once said, "Bette, Keep on truckin'." So I intend to go on writing—whether it's magazine articles, stories for volunteer organizations, or even finally to begin the Lake Minnetonka mystery that I have long wanted to do.

Having cruised Lake Minnetonka many times aboard our family motorboat, the Blue Note, I have observed many architectural losses: namely some of our best examples of residential design. These include the Philip Pillsbury house designed by Ralph Rapson, late dean of the University of Minnesota's School of Architecture; the Dayton/Burnet house by Romaldo Guirgola, famed for his modernist style; The Sweat house by Edwin Lundie, long esteemed Minnesota architect with a Scandinavian attitude; the glamorous Pillsbury estate Southways, originally designed by Harry T. Lindeberg, later restored by Beyer Blinder Belle and now completely destroyed; and one of the oldest, the Northrup house designed by William Channing Whitney in his sweeping classical manner. It all strikes me as a disturbing trend—tearing down perfectly designed timely homes in favor of building new extravaganzas. What will be next, I wonder? Fortunately, there's another hopeful trend: the increasing numbers of contemporary homes appear-

ing on the lakeshore; homes by such architects as Julie Snow, Petersen/Keller Architects and Charles Stinson. What will happen next on our lake? I hope you and my sailing friends will take note and help support historic preservation.

Susan, skipper or crew member, loves sailing.

Since writing this memoir, while holed up in my cozy apartment at Folkstone in Wayzata, I want to encourage other seniors to get busy and write their life stories for their grandchildren. No one else can do it for you. In my case, I really wanted my family to learn why I entered the Journalism School at the University of Minnesota, and how that experience pointed the way into my varied and gratifying career.

In order to squeeze in these multiple jobs, I've condensed portions of my personal life. Those are fully related in a separate memoir for my family only—"Grams Journal." I've found that it's fun to write about oneself. Now it's your turn.

— Bette Jones Hammel
August 2, 2018

From 1993 ro 2017, Bette Hammel covered architecture in articles for Minnesota AIA (American Institute of Architects) describing architects and their projects ranging from libraries, churches, colleges, and art centers to civic buildings, museums, schools, and especially homes. Her articles also appeared in *Architecture Minnesota, Midwest Home Design*, and *Architectural Record of New York*, featuring leading architects such as Joan Soranno and John Cook of HGA for the Walker Art Center's vastly improved new entry, Gar Hargens of Close Associates for his modern home designs, John Cunningham's lifetime of outstanding work for the entertainment industry, and Rafferty & Rafferty for outstanding churches. "I just can't stop writing about our local architects and the importance of the work they do," she says.

The Minnesota AIA has presented Bette with two special awards for enhancing the public's understanding of the vital role architecture plays in our community. She is the author of *From Bauhaus to Bowties, Legendary Homes of Lake Minnetonka, Legendary Homes of the Minneapolis Lakes*, and *Wild About Architecture*, and she also contributed substantially to *Great Houses of Summit Avenue and the Hill District*. She lives in Wayzata, Minnesota.